# OLD GLASS CO.,

19 95

**...cturers,**

**...D OFFICE,**

**...PITTSBURGH, PA.**

**...dville, Pa.**

**...SPECIALTY.**

**...NIGHT LAMP.**
...rations—½ Scale.

**NO. 51 LAMP AND 8 1-2 INCH SHADE.**
Bisque Finish. Decorations Nos. 614, 615 and 616—Scale ¼.

# THE EVOLUTION OF THE NIGHT LAMP

Ann Gilbert McDonald, Ph.D.

Wallace-Homestead Book Co.
1912 Grand
Des Moines, Iowa 50305

ISBN 0-87069-270-4
Library of Congress Catalog
No. 79-63057

Photography by Glen Leach

Published by

Wallace Homestead Book Co.
1912 Grand Avenue
Des Moines, Iowa 50305

# Table of Contents

# Dedication

To Claire, Bradley and Margaret Teresa with gratitude and love.

Kirsten Bergquist with The Defender Night Lamp

# Introduction

Several years ago, I purchased a collection of night lamps from my neighbor who was moving from her home to an apartment. In the collection were two Bullseye lamps, a clear Cosmos and a Reflecting Fans lamp. I recall wondering at that time what companies made these dainty lamps. My curiosity grew as my collection enlarged. Four years ago, I decided to accept the challenge and to find the companies. What a challenge it was: hundreds of trade journals to search through page by page, dozens of catalogs and books on lighting and glass companies to peruse. Pictures of lamps in trade journal ads and lamp catalogs made it possible to identify nearly 200 lamps. Most lamps were given names by their makers, such as the Sylvan Night Lamp or the Dixie, and these names are provided here, as well as the Smith numbers from Frank and Ruth Smith's book, *Miniature Lamps.*

Identifying lamps and companies, while beneficial to the collector wishing to date his lamp and to know its maker, was not my only aim. I know the importance of such individual glassmakers as Nicholas Kopp, and the glass companies, and I have sought to provide a history of the night lamp from the Betty lamp to the modern night lamps reproduced by the L. G. Wright Company.

To set up the color photos took skill, imagination and the aid of several generous persons. Gail Bergquist dressed her two-year-old daughter, Kirsten, in the lovely period dress belonging to Charlotte Pranger, combed her hair in 1890's style, put her in little, white tights and coached her on how to approach the night lamp. Kirsten's picture appears on the opposite page. The Victorian dressing table shown in the center of the book featured period accessories from Ruth Glover and Elsie McLaughlin. Elsie also loaned the new, green Fleur-de-Lis lamp and the Acorn lamp. Helen Sandeen personally carried her lovely lamps to my home to be photographed in color and black and white.

With great goodwill, Dolores Burke allowed me to borrow several of her precious night lamps to photograph for the book: Smith 4, 12, 31, 78, 109, 148, 292, the All Night Lamp and the Ribbed Pedestal lamp. To her and to Ruth Krogh, who loaned the Imperial Number 9 lamp and the Vapo-Cresolene box, I am most grateful.

Mary Jane Clark generously brought two lamps, the Plain Windows and the Little Jewel lamps, all the way from her home in the west to the Smiths' home where we photographed them. A large "thank you" goes to her and to Helen Feltner. I drove 70 miles to Helen's home and borrowed four lamps: the Primrose, S 105, 293 and 419. With great joy, I discovered that Helen had the rare Primrose lamp by

Gillinder, since very few exist. She also informed me where I could find and buy George Duncan's Narrow Swirl night lamp. Her aid was invaluable! Ruth Oland kindly allowed us to photograph the following lamps: the Acme, the Apple Blossom, the handled Daisy, the Moon and Star, and the milk glass Fire-Fly. Ruth has collected night lamps for more than 30 years, and revealed that her husband's aunt received the Nellie Bly and other night lamps as Christmas gifts when she was a child.

Special tribute goes to the Northern Virginia Antique Arts Association. To this group I first gave the lecture on night lamps which grew into an article for *The Antique Trader Weekly* in June, 1977, and finally into this book. I salute the founder of the Antique Arts Association, Orva Heissenbuttel, and thank her for the page of Miniature Lamps from the A.A. Importing Catalog, for information on glass companies and for recommending a photographer for the book. I also wish to thank members Ruth Glover, Helen Sandeen and Charlotte Thomas for their help. Charlotte let me borrow several rare lamps to photograph for the book, as well as books on lighting.

A bouquet of gratitude goes to Frank and Ruth Smith for the information they shared, for permission to photograph some of their lamps and to use the Smith numbers in this book, and for their gracious hospitality during two very pleasant visits. The following lamps from the Smiths' collection appear here: S 11, VII, 12, 13, 15, 20, 22, 23, 32, 51, 52, 54, 55, 57, 59, 77, 83, 92, 108, 115, 116, 118, 121, 132, 133, 144-147, 150, 167, 173, 184, 186, 189, 190-192, 200, 201, 203, 211, 214, 217-220, 222, 228, 231, 241, 257, 266, 272-275, 279, 281, 282, 284, 285, 292, 294, 299, 302, 308, 309, 310, 316, 323, 324, 326, 330, 331, 374, 380, 381, 383-386, 388-390, 393-396, 398-400, 431, 432, 439, 445, 470, 471, 475, 477, 478, 480, 482, 491, 512, 513, 579, 586, 601, 626, the Time Lamp, the Dixie, the Delft, the Dresden, Wright's Daisy and Cube, the Fairy Night Lamp and the English cameo glass lamp. I am most grateful to the Smiths and to all the generous collectors who shared their lamps and information about them.

I am listing here in the Introduction the lamps and the persons who loaned them, rather than putting these names under the photos of the lamps. Why do this? First, some persons prefer to loan their lamps anonymously. Secondly, some of the lamp groupings represent several owners; for example, one photo has four lamps from three different owners. Some of the lamps and period accessories pictured here come from my own collection. At times, readers will find lamps mentioned in the text without an accompanying photo. Unfortunately, some lamps were unavailable to photograph. Readers can check the Smiths' book, Catherine Thuro's *Oil Lamps* or *Crockery and Glass Journal* for photos of these lamps.

Norma Jenkins, Associate Librarian of the Corning Museum of Glass Library, assisted me in many ways. She found several source books and trade journal articles, particularly on Nail City Stamping Company, duplicated them and sent them to me, pointing out new areas for research. On her busiest day, the dedication of the new museum, she welcomed me to read microfilm for eight hours, had the machine and films all set out and reference books at my desk! To her and to Virginia Wright, I send a large "thank you"!

In response to my request in *The Trader*, several persons took photos of their lamps and sent them to me. I am most grateful to: the Kenneth Fishers for the photo of the opaline lamp; R. Wayne Hall for the Brass Double Student lamp; Dean Langness for photos of the Jr. Rochester, Cottage and Fireside lamps; Arthur Ronat for S 64, S 110, the McFaddin Glow lamp, the Atterbury Prism lamp and others. Richard Shryock and Elizabeth Trudell sent photos of student lamps and U.S. Glass figural lamps, respectively.

Reprints of catalogs were graciously provided by J.W. Courter and Dr. David Portman. J.W. Courter sent the Plume and Atwood catalog of 1906, while Dr. Portman sent reprints of the Rochester Lamp Company and Bradley and Hubbard catalogs, courtesy of The Gilded Age Press, Washington Mills, New York.

Catherine Thuro and William Heacock graciously shared pages from the U.S. Glass Company and Fostoria catalogs with me. Their books on *Oil Lamps* and *Victorian Colored Pattern Glass*, respectively, provided direction and inspiration. Dorla Battersby provided information on the L.G. Wright lamps and other new miniature lamps.

A special tribute goes to Glen Leach, the photographer for this book. With infinite patience and care, he positioned each lamp and shifted numerous lights around to capture such tiny titles as Buttercup or Firefly. In a burst of genius, he was able to photograph the spider web on the Robin Hood lamp—a detail not easily seen with the eye. Always cheerful and encouraging, he worked long hours through the hot summer to obtain these clear and detailed photographs.

All quotations from *The Crockery and Glass Journal* are reprinted here with the

3

kind permission of the current owner of the copyright, the publisher of *Gifts and Tableware*.

Abbreviations are used throughout the book for the titles of the trade journals. A key to these abbreviations follows:

Abbreviations of Trade Journals

| | |
|---|---|
| C & G | Crockery and Glass Journal |
| CGL | China, Glass and Lamps |
| HF | House Furnisher |
| HW | The Housewife |
| PGR | Pottery and Glassware Reporter |
| PGBS | Pottery, Glass and Brass Salesman |

# Chapter I
# The Earliest Night Lamps

Today the phrase, "night lamp," suggests a small electric lamp on a child's bureau, which softens the darkness and quells fears. Before the age of electricity, such primitive lighting devices as the Betty Lamp, the whale oil lamp or the small kerosene lamp chased the ghosts away. One of the earliest night lamps was the sparking lamp, which was hand-made, shaped and blown by the glassmaker shortly after 1800. By 1890, the glassmaker had become adept at pressing glass, embossing, painting and decorating his tiny lamps. He could produce myriad effects in his colorful opaline, amberina, cameo, satin and milk glass miniature lamps. These we collect and cherish today.

It is my aim to trace the evolution of the night lamp from the Pilgrims to modern times. What are night lamps? They are lamps from two to 12 inches tall, with an average height of eight inches and a base diameter of one and one-half to three inches. They lighted the way to bed, and furnished a small beacon during the night to comfort a child or to solace a sick person. What companies made them? Most large glassmakers produced with pride a line of night lamps, from the early, clear glass blown lamps of the Sandwich Glass Company to the delicate, milk glass ones of Consolidated Lamp and Glass Company.

I have endeavored to discover the companies that made the most beautiful and graceful examples of the night light, and to provide in the following pages photos and company attributions, as well as histories of the most prominent companies. All the lighting devices in this chapter, from the Betty lamp to the early whale oil lamps, were made available by Charlotte Thomas, who has a fine collection of early lighting.

The history of the night lamp in America dates back to Pilgrim times. The Pilgrims brought a primitive lighting device with them on the Mayflower from England, the Betty lamp. Related to the Betty was the Crusie, a pear-shaped flat lamp with a pointed channel holding the wick. Made of iron and supported by a curved hanger, the open reservoir Crusie lamp was one of the earliest ever invented. Like the Crusie, the Betty lamp was pear-shaped, but it was often covered and had a raised wick support. This half-round wick support was attached to the bottom of the lamp and did not touch the sides, allowing the wick to stay above the nose of the lamp so the oil would drip back into the reservoir. Made in one piece of cast or wrought iron, the Betty, like the Crusie, had a curving hanger to hold or hang it. As time went by, the Betty was made also in pewter, tin, copper and brass. The wick consisted of twisted rag, hemp or rope, and the oil used for fuel was a malodorous fish oil.

The Betty and the Crusie lamps

In the one-room Pilgrim log cabins with upper lofts for sleeping, the Betty lamp, made by the village blacksmith, was indispensable, for it could be carried in the hand, hung from a rafter or a chair back, put on a table or stuck into the log wall or into a hole in the stone fireplace. At bedtime, it was carried upstairs and stuck in a crack in the wall. As the earliest lighting device used by the Pilgrims, the Betty lamps are a fascinating precursor to the night lamp, though they gave little light and smelled awful. They were used until the 1850's.

From the primitive, open-reservoir lamps, such as the Crusie and the Betty, one proceeds to the closed reservoir or font oil lamps, often made of glass. "Just as the slanted wick support, typical of the Betty lamp, marked a major improvement over the Crusie, so John Miles' 1787 English patent of an agitable lamp with a threaded burner and sealed upright wick tube brought an end to widespread use of the Betty and its allies. The use of a vertical wick tube supported by a metal disc isolated the flame, and this made possible the entry of the glass blower and his heat-sensitive product into the lamp business. He could produce the glass fonts to be filled with whale oil," wrote Lawrence Cooke in *Lighting in America*, p.45.

Pewter Camphene Lamp, Lard Oil Wick Tube, and Lard Oil Lamp

Pressed spark lamp or hand lamp with single drop burner, pewter collar and applied handle

Peg Lamp

Peg Lamp in Candlestick Holder

Instead of a piece of rag or hemp, there now was the drop burner, a tin disc with a wick tube that rested on the opening in the font. The cork burner succeeded the drop burner and was more secure; it had one or two wick tubes soldered to a top plate with a cork wafer beneath that fit into the neck of the lamp. The last improvement in whale oil burners for glass lamps was the threaded metal collar attached to the straight neck on the glass font, which allowed burners to be transferred from metal to glass lamps. Whale oil, camphene and lard oil supplanted the malodorous fish oil for fuel. There was an abundance of whale oil, especially sperm oil. Early whale oil lamps used the drop burner. As whale oil grew more expensive, lard oil rendered from the fat of the pig took its place. Lard oil was thick and tended to congeal in cold weather. Copper wick tubes for the lard oil lamp reached down into the font to conduct the heat and to keep the lard oil melted.

A volatile fuel, camphene caused many accidents. The wick tubes of the camphene lamp were long, angled away from each other and stood above the font. Wick tube caps prevented evaporation and fires. The tubes did not proceed down into the font like the lard oil tubes because of the danger of fire. Whale oil lamps often were converted to use lard or camphene.

This long explanation about open and closed reservoir lamps, from the Crusie to the Betty to the whale oil, lard oil and camphene lamps serves as an introduction to the glass lighting devices, made by the neophyte glassblowers of the early 1800's. In the evolution of the night lamp, the following lamps played an important role: the peg lamp, the wine glass lamp, the blown chamber lamp, the stopper mold lamp, the small stand lamp with cup plate base, and the pressed and molded spark lamp. The earliest glass lamp, the peg lamp, circa 1825, was made to sit in a candlestick or holder, as it could not stand alone. Made of blown glass with a pointed end, it could be moved from room to room like the Betty lamp and put into a waiting candlestick, chandelier or wooden holder mounted on the wall.

From the peg lamp to the wine glass lamp was a short step for the inventive glassmaker. He looked at the wine glass he was blowing and imagined it as a lamp. By pulling its rim over to make a font and leaving a small opening at the top for the wick holder, he created the wine glass lamp. These lamps had an applied knop stem and a circular base. Most measured under six inches; many were only four inches high. They burned whale oil, and had a tin cap burner with one or two wick holders. With their baluster shapes, these little lamps looked exactly like wine glasses and were used to light the way to bed.

In the 1820's, the New England Glass Company, Sandwich Glass and Bakewell, Page and Bakewell all offered glass lamps: button stem lamps, chamber and stand lamps. Button stem or wine glass lamps were mentioned in Deming Jarves' Account Book at Sandwich in 1825 and were small chamber lights with baluster stems, hand blown as we have seen. Chamber lamps were usually hand blown also and often had handles. Both chamber and wine glass lamps were made quickly by the glassmaker and sold cheaply. Most had cork disc burners. Following them came the pressed or molded spark lamps 1835-1850, usually burning whale oil, though some burned camphene. They were fluted or slightly molded lamps and had collars for screw thread burners. Often they shone with bright colors, such as sapphire blue, green or amethyst.

The stopper mold lamp was a unique invention. These lamps were blown in three-part molds for decanter stoppers. Then the stopper stem was removed and the opening shaped for the burner. The original top of the stopper was flattened as a base and a handle was applied to complete the lamp, as Willard Keyes describes it in "Miniature Glass Lamps."

Wine Glass Lamp with Matching Wine Glass

From 1830 to 1840, small stand lamps appeared with clear blown fonts and cup plate bases. These bases were pressed in the molds of the early cup plates, but the bases were thicker than the cup plates and the plates were inverted so the bottom side of the cup plate became the top of the lamp base. The cup plate was attached to the free blown font by a wafer of glass to make a handsome lamp, as illustrated here. For more information on the early lighting devices, such as the wine glass lamp or the spark lamp, the reader may refer to Lura Woodside Watkins' "American Glass Lamps," in *Antiques* or in *Lighting in America*, the main source used for this chapter.

By 1860, kerosene, an inexpensive fuel refined from petroleum, took the place of the other lamp fuels. After 1860, certain lamps were made specifically to burn kerosene: the pressed glass lamps, pressed in a mold in patterns such as Bullseye and Diamond Point, Cable, Harp, Thumbprint, Star and Punty, Moon and Star. They came in inverted bell shapes, and had a bell tone from the flint in the glass. Many had handles and were used as chamber lamps. As demand grew for pressed lamps, so grew the glass industry which made the lamps.

Stopper Mold Lamp

Why do we call these early glass and metal chamber lamps night lamps? Research shows they were used mainly in bedrooms. Small hand lamps were carried to the bedroom, put on the bedside table or candlestand and frequently left to burn all night. Miss Leslie's Housebook, Philadelphia, 1840, recommended: "Small

Sandwich Cup Plate Lamp

Sandwich Blown Chamber Lamp with pressed base

japanned lamps are most convenient for carrying up and down stairs, and for lighting to bed. . . . Every evening before dusk, as many of these bed-lamps as may be wanted by the members of the family, should be arranged on a japanned waiter, with a brass lamp of a larger size burning in the middle, and a few paper matches placed on one side. The waiter of lamps should be kept on a small table at the first landing place of the stairs or in a recess or retired part of the hall or entry below." With a tray of night lamps ready at the bottom of the stairs, each family member could pick up his own lamp and carry it to his own room. Miss Leslie commended night lamps: "There are a variety of lamps for burning all night in chambers; an excellent custom, which frequently prevents much inconvenience particularly in cases of sudden illness. In every house it is well to have a lamp burning the whole night, in at least one of the rooms." (*Lighting in America*, p. 78).

Pertinent to this history of the night lamp are notes from a lecture my grandmother, Hester Gilbert, gave her antiques club in 1949. I am fortunate to have her notes and will quote from them. She wrote, "My earliest realization of lamps dates back to very early childhood. We never had a light at night at my mother's and father's, but a great deal of my life was spent at my grandmother's and there was always a night light there. These little night lights, as they were called, held for one a fascination that has lasted down through the years. Long after kerosene lamps and then gas and electricity came into every day use, I longed at night for the tiny glimmer of the little sperm oil or lard oil lamp. Living on a farm in the Mohawk Valley as a child, lard oil was well known to me. Many times I have watched my grandmother and her housekeeper put into small stone jars the yellowish oil left after the pure white lard had drained all night . . . Even when in later years there was no need of saving that refuse, the thrift of a good housewife prevailed, just in case a bad blizzard arrived before the kerosene wagon did."

My grandmother had two peg lamps in her collection and pointed to them as she talked: "The two small sperm lights with the protruding stems were interchangeable, used in either candlesticks or in heavy bottles. Mother Gilbert told me both were in use when she came as a bride to North Branford in 1863. Mother said when you just wanted to light a room, you put the light in a tall bottle. When you wanted to read or sew or write you put it in a candlestick or in a low bottle." Finally, referring to one lamp, my grandmother said, "The tiny one with the white globe Mother Gilbert kept on her bureau at night when her first child was a baby in 1865."

I quote from Hester Gilbert's notes at length to give an idea of the fascinating and diverse uses of these early lamps, and also to prove that the smallest lamps were used as night lamps. Most scholars agree that the tiny lamps were not used for courting, as the term spark lamp suggests. Instead, they were used to guide someone up the stairs and to light his way to bed. As we have seen, some night lamps burned all night in a child's or a sick person's room.

The small whale oil lamps which evolved into the pressed glass chamber lamps are the ancestors of our own miniature lamps. I prefer to call the miniature lamps "night lamps," since this is what they were called from the nineteenth through the early twentieth centuries in conversation, in journals and in trade catalogs put out by the glass companies.

"Night lamps have grown remarkably in popularity in the last two or three years, and no well-regulated house can afford to be without them," wrote a critic on "The Lamp Trade," in CGL on May 13, 1891. Indeed, night lamps were used not only in bedrooms, but also in bathrooms, living rooms and all over the house. In the 1890's, the lamps were collected and displayed. "It is the fashion now to have lamps for decorative purposes," wrote a commentator on "The Lamp Trade," in C & G, April 21, 1898, "and while that fashion lasts, the fashionable woman will put lamps in all sorts of places. It is getting to be a fad to have a collection of lamps just as it is to collect souvenir spoons or A.D. coffees." Before 1860, two or three lamps sufficed in one household, but by 1892 many more were needed. "Every household requires for its comfort from three to a dozen lamps of various grades and styles, and it therefore becomes clearly evident that the proportions of the demand for these goods is truly enormous," wrote PGR, September 15, 1892.

Brass Whale Oil Chamber lamp

The apogee of night lamp production occurred in the 1890's, and the lamps produced were spectacular with decorated, embossed milk glass, and delicately ribbed, enameled colored glass. They sold for ten cents to a dollar each. Hence the Victorian housewife could build a handsome collection of night lamps quite inexpensively. "Then again, our lamp men are making their goods so cheap and so attractive, that thousands of lamps are bought more for show and ornament than for purposes of illumination. Many a lamp is bought because it is pretty, and is about as cheap a way of 'showing off' as modern pretense has yet evolved," wrote PGR in "The Lamp Season of 1892," April 14, 1892. The housewife used night lamps to decorate her living room, to provide light for her desk and dressing table. As shown in the color photo in the center of the book, night lamps on the dressing table illuminated the lady's toilette and served as graceful, decorative accessories.

Why was there such demand for lamps of all kinds? An article in PGR, April 14, 1892, attributes this to increased population from immigration, the expanding of industry and the increase of population in the cities, the greater height of the buildings, the habit of reading a daily paper, the growth of modern periodicals, reviews and class journals which the merchant, mechanic and businessman had to read in the evenings. All these led to the demand for more lamps. By 1892, $25,000,000 was involved in lamp manufacture, with the low price of petroleum spurring increase in production, as oil was 8¢ to 10¢ a gallon! Oil lamps were cheaper and brighter than gas lamps, noted PGR, February 18, 1892.

This boom in oil lamp production continued through the turn of the century and only electricity dimmed its success. By 1908, the glass companies turned to making electric light fixtures. By 1920, the main buyers of oil lamps were in the country. Fewer lamps were sold in the cities because of widespread use of gas and electricity. Surprisingly, however, kerosene lamps were still selling well in 1913 at the Pittsburgh Exposition, according to C & G, June 23, 1913.

From the Betty lamp in the Pilgrim upper loft to the whale oil lamp glimmering on the candlestand to the dainty miniature oil lamp on the Victorian dressing table, the night lamp grew and thrived over the centuries. Used in the bedroom, the bath, the hall, to ornament the house or to service the sick room, the night lamp proved indispensable.

The Atterbury Shoe lamp

The Log Cabin lamp by Atterbury

The Atterbury Prism lamp

# Chapter II

# Early Kerosene Night Lamps: Atterbury, Olmstead, Bristol Brass

In the period from 1865 to 1885, some primitive but unique night lamps appeared: the Log Cabin and Shoe lamps of Atterbury and Company, and Little Harry's Night Lamp of L.H. Olmstead with its numerous imitators: The Little Pet, Little Favorite, Firefly and Little Crown night lamps.

Atterbury and Company of Pittsburgh made a few night lamps using a unique four-part mold patented June 30, 1868. Pictured and described in Catherine Thuro's *Oil Lamps*, the lower part of the mold below the shoulder comprised the handle matrix and font. First, molten glass was put into the handle matrix. A gather of glass then went into the font, the upper portion of the mold was closed and the glass was blown to finish the font and handle. From this mold came the Log Cabin and the Shoe lamps. Based upon this patent information, we can assign the Log Cabin (S 50) and the Shoe (S 51) lamps to Atterbury and Company. In the collection of Arthur Ronat is a handsome Atterbury Prism pattern night lamp, authenticated by Thuro, 89h, and shown here.

L.H. Olmstead of New York, patentee and sole manufacturer of Little Harry's Night Lamp, was the inventor who introduced the night lamp with the clear glass base, opal chimney and Olmstead burner. His lamp was copied by numerous other manufacturers. A front page ad in *Crockery and Glass Journal* on April 12, 1877, heralded the arrival of Little Harry's Night Lamp and praised its chimney and shade combined in one, its two-ounce weight and its ability to burn 12 hours. The font was made from flint glass and the trademark "Little Harry's Night Lamp" was blown into each font. As shown here, the tiny lamp was fully identified by embossing on the back: L.H. Olmstead, Pat. March 20, 1877, New York. This lamp, Fig. 15 from the Smiths' collection, stands 3½" high and represents the prototype of the early kerosene night lamp. Olmstead also offered this as a bracket lamp, a hand lamp with brass base and reflector, a hand lamp with applied handle as in S 13, and in a tiny cobalt blue lamp. All had the trade mark, Little Harry's Night Lamp.

Imitators of the Little Harry abounded: the Little Pet Night Lamp, the Little Wonder and many more. The Little Pet was produced by W. Fichtenberg of New York. It looked just like Little Harry's Night Lamp, but its burner was raised higher, almost on a tripod, as shown in the ad in C & G, June 28, 1877, and the chimney shade came in varied colors.

The Little Wonder and The Little Favorite (S 16) were both retailed by C.S. Raymond and were tiny hand lamps with opal chimneys like the Little Harry. C.S.

Raymond of New York also manufactured the Wonder, Vesta, Imperial, Brilliant and Crown lamps, as well as a miniature brass student lamp, mentioned in C & G, October 3, 1878. The Little Favorite came as a standing lamp with the name embossed on the pedestal base, and as a hand lamp with applied handle, both shown here. Each one had an opal chimney shade and an Olmstead type burner. Sometimes the lamp was called The Improved Favorite.

The Little Gem Night Lamp was offered in May, 1877, by Samuel Clark of New York in *Crockery and Glass Journal.* It closely resembled Little Harry's Night

Little Harry's Night Lamps S 15 and S 13 by L. H. Olmstead

The Little Favorite hand and stand lamps by C. S. Raymond

The Fire-Fly lamp

Lamp. Indeed, Clark boasts, "Since putting my lamp on the market there has been malicious persons publishing foolish threats of prosecution to everybody who sells any lamp but their own. I would only state that this is done for the simple reason that I beat them in price. My lamp infringes on nobody's patent, and I PROMISE TO PROTECT anyone who buys and sells my lamp." With bad grammar and bravado he defies all competitors. Indeed, his lamp duplicates almost exactly Little Harry's Night Lamp, but it has The Little Gem embossed on the font. Clark also sold The Little Crown Night Lamp, a standing lamp with an embossed base, ribbed pedestal and ringed font, June, 1877, in C & G.

F.H. Lovell and Company and the Bristol Brass and Clock Company advertised several fine night lamps in C & G in 1877. They made the famous Firefly lamps, S 6,7,8,9. These included a small lamp with the embossed word "Firefly" on the font, a handled lamp, a bracket lamp and a handsome chandelier with two to four lights, with a height of 12 inches and a spread of 12 inches. One precious ad for the Firefly lamp, June 14, 1877, showed the lamp on the back between the wings of a real firefly and included this poem, "But oft from the Indian Hunter's Camp, / This Lover and maid so true, / Are seen at the hour of midnight damp, / To cross the Lake by a FIRE-FLY LAMP, / And paddle their white canoe."

By himself, F.H. Lovell promoted the Wide Awake hand lamp with a clear glass font, the embossed words "Wide Awake," a nutmeg burner and chimney and an applied handle in November, 1878, in C & G. On its own, the Bristol Brass and Clock Company in 1878 and 1879 developed brass night lamps such as the New Student Night Lamp (S 83), a very tiny lamp only slightly over seven inches high, advertised in C & G, April 12, 1878. The Magic Brass Night Lamp was offered May 1, 1879, and resembled the Cottage Lamp of Plume and Atwood shown in Chapter VII.

Returning to 1877, we find the Empire Night Lamp leading the field, touted month after month in C & G. A clear glass lamp with the embossed word "Empire," it was probably made by the Empire State Flint Glass Works of Brooklyn, although both that company and M. Prescott advertised it. Coming with or without an applied handle, it was advertised from January, 1878 to 1881. "Turned low it makes an excellent Night Lamp; turned high a lamp to read by, to go around the house with, for the hall, the nursery, the sick room. . . .", *Pottery and Glassware Reporter* noted May 5, 1881. Its companion was the Union Night Lamp which was offered by M. Prescott as early as October 25, 1877, in C & G. Both lamps had a burner with a rotating lid to permit pouring the kerosene into the lamp.

The milk glass Fire-Fly lamp S 9 by Bristol Brass and Lovell

The Empire Night Lamp

The New Student Night Lamp by Bristol Brass

The Time and Light Lamp by Bristol Brass

Toy Stand Lamps by Storm Brothers

Storm Brothers, glass manufacturers of Philadelphia, Pa., made the prettiest pair of early kerosene lamps called Toy Stand Lamps (S 11). They were the only early night lamps with colorful blue or white pedestal bases. Measuring 7″ high to the top of the shade, they were pictured in C & G, October 11, 1877, with Olmstead type burners, clear glass patterned fonts, colored bases and opal shades.

Empire State Flint Glass Works and Nicholas Wapler offered The Matchless Night Lamp. On June 28, 1877, it appeared in C & G as a flat octagonal lamp with the embossed title "Matchless," a raised Olmstead burner and opal chimney. Boasting that its detachable ratchet burner was a model of simplicity and perfection, it also had the revolving feeder cap like that in the Empire Night Lamp. The Improved Matchless Night Lamp offered in October, 1877, by Nicholas Wapler of New York differed considerably from its predecessor. The Improved Matchless came in two styles: (1) a squatty lamp with dots, squiggles and the embossed title; (2) a tall, handsome stand lamp with ribbed pedestal and embossed Matchless font. On November 8, 1877, all three Matchless night lamps were pictured on the front page of *Crockery and Glass Journal,* and competitors were notified not to infringe the patent for the feeder cap.

Manhattan Brass Company made the Twilight Night Lamp (S 19), a stand lamp with a vertical ribbed font and a base titled "Twilight," and promoted it October 25, 1877, in C & G. They also manufactured The Little Joker, another duplicate of Little Harry's Night Lamp, and handsome brass student lamps. They received the Centennial Medal of Merit for their wares.

Finally, among the imitators of L.H. Olmstead was Edward Rorke and Company of New York who made the Evening Star lamps, (S 12). These featured clear glass fonts with or without applied handles, the poetic title "Evening Star" and Olmstead type burners. My little Evening Star has a gorgeous firey opalescent milk glass shade and on the base is embossed "E.R. and Company." It is a joy to own such a tiny (2½″ high) example of the glassmaker's art.

The Evening Star by Rorke

Several of these early lamps were unavailable to photograph. Persons who wish to see photos may check *Crockery and Glass Journal* from 1877 to 1881, where all these lamps are advertised and pictured.

Several Time lamps were made. The Grand-Val Time Indicating Lamp Company of New York offered one for sale in C & G, January 6, 1881. This lamp had

The Time Lamp by Grand-Val

the words "Time Lamp" embossed on the base and had a scale of hours on its glass cylinder font. Used in the bedroom and in the sick room, the lamp was adept at "Silently recording each fleeting hour, yet avoiding the monotonous ticking of a clock so annoying to the invalid," the ad claimed. The Bristol Brass and Clock Company of New York made the Time and Light Lamp (S 23) and advertised it in C & G, May 5, 1881. With its opal beehive shade, this lamp had the words "Time and Light Pride of America" embossed on the base.

The lamps of the 1865-1885 period were simple, clear glass, with Olmstead type burners and opal chimneys. Often they had names embossed on the font, such as "Twilight" or "Little Pet." A few, like the Atterbury lamps or the Toy Stand lamps, were unique and creative and foreshadowed the glorious decades to come.

The Santa Claus, the Rose and the Cone lamps by Fostoria Shade and Lamp

Two Acme and three Rose lamps by Fostoria Shade and Consolidated

# Chapter III
# Consolidated Lamp and Glass Company

The peak of production for night lamps was from 1880 to 1920, when the glassmakers unleashed their latent creativity with a lavish array of colors, shapes and finishes from bright red satin glass to creamy embossed milk glass, from delicate English cameo glass to iridescent Tiffany Favrile. Never have the little lamps looked so pretty, so feminine, so desirable! Moreover, everyone could afford to own one, since they sold for only a dime or a quarter, an amazing fact to those collectors who pay $150 to $800 for those same lamps today!

It has been a long journey from those primitive, open-reservoir lamps made of wrought iron, to the simple clear glass Little Harry lamps, to the sophisticated milk glass and colored satin glass lamps of the 1890's. The glass companies vied with each other to see who could produce the most, the prettiest, the cheapest. One of the largest and most successful companies was Consolidated Lamp and Glass Company of Fostoria, Ohio, and later Coraopolis, Pennsylvania. Its predecessor was the Fostoria Shade and Lamp Company.

The Fostoria Shade and Lamp Company of Fostoria, Ohio, not to be confused with the Fostoria Glass Company, made many night lamps, including the enchanting figural Santa Claus lamp produced in 1892. Advertised in PGR, November 17, 1892, that lamp instantly enjoyed great popularity. It was used as an ornament on the mantle, in the bedroom and on the Christmas tree and sold for $4.00 a dozen, a great bargain compared to today's price of $1,200! Fostoria Shade also made other night lamps in the pre-1894 period, including "Erminie" which came in white, turquoise, marine and rose, "The Quilt Caster," and "The Rose". All came complete with shades and in many gay colors, as advertised in PGR, November 24, 1892.

Melvin Murray's *History of Fostoria, Ohio Glass 1887-1920* provides a detailed history of the Fostoria Shade and Lamp Company. It was established in Fostoria, Ohio, in 1890, under the direction of Nicholas Kopp, formerly with the Hobbs Glass Company of Wheeling. Building of the factory began in March, 1890, with completion that spring. It seems beyond dispute that many of the colorful night lamps later offered by Consolidated Lamp and Glass Company were produced first under Kopp's aegis at Fostoria Shade and Lamp, and later made at this same factory after the merger of Fostoria Shade and Consolidated. Thus, most of the lamps that Consolidated sold in 1894-95 were Kopp-inspired and made in Fostoria.

Nicholas Kopp was only 25 when he became manager of the Fostoria Shade plant, and he already had patents for several of his glass inventions. Besides the famous Santa Claus Lamp (Smith VII), Kopp also made the lovely Rose night lamp (S 385), advertised October 9, 1890, in C & G. By September 1, 1892, Kopp had won renown for his company and publicity in C & G: "This company have made a specialty of rich colored lamps, and have brought out a large line of figured shades and cylinders . . . in rose, canary, turquoise, pearl grey and marine. Mr. Kopp, the company's designer and metal maker, has an enviable reputation for his designs and color effects. This year he has eclipsed all previous records, and his chaste Rococo designs are very beautiful, being new, attractive and novel. Among this company's best sellers at the present time are their night lamps, Nos. 02 and 800." Probably No. 2 was S 389, and No. 800 was S 394, the Cone lamp.

An 1892 ad in C & G featured the Cone pattern in a syrup, sugar, creamer, etc. Undoubtedly, a Cone night lamp also was made at Fostoria Shade. Indeed, it was advertised in 1894 by Consolidated as Night Lamp 800, the same number it had at Fostoria Shade. The famous 1894 ad in *China, Glass and Lamps* which Kamm shows in Book VI, plate 81, and which appeared July 4, pictured six lamps probably made first by Kopp at Fostoria Shade and Lamp and later re-offered by Consolidated.

The Consolidated Lamp and Glass Company dated back to 1855, when it was called Wallace McAfee Co. Ltd., according to Marie Robinson in a March, 1974, article in *Spinning Wheel*. The first item in the trade journals concerning Consolidated occurred December 20, 1893, in CGL in an announcement of the merger of Consolidated Lamp and Glass: "The sale of the plant of the Fostoria Shade and Lamp Co., of Pittsburgh, was concluded on December 13. . . . It is the largest factory manufacturing lamps and lamp shades in the United States. The principal stockholders are W.C. Brown and J.B. Graham, of Fostoria. The new company has a paid-up capital of $200,000, and will largely increase the plant, which is already employing 250 people." The news of the merger indicated that Consolidated was already operating at Pittsburgh prior to 1893. An ad in CGL, February 28, 1894, corroborated the fact that Consolidated had succeeded Fostoria Shade and Wallace McAfee: "Consolidated Lamp and Glass Company, Successors to Fostoria Shade and Lamp Co. and Wallace McAfee, Co. Ltd." The new company offered "Decorated and Art Colored Lamps, Salts, Peppers and Novelties in Colored Glass."

Nicholas Kopp managed the Fostoria plant of Consolidated Lamp, putting out a large assortment of night lamps, and making iridescent glass, cased, satin and optic glass in a variety of colors such as turquoise, canary, blue and rose. The Fostoria Shade and Lamp factory, run by Kopp before and after the merger with Consolidated, operated night and day at peak production.

In 1896, the entire Consolidated operation moved to Coraopolis, Pennsylvania. In a front page ad in CGL, March 25, 1896, they announced: "Having outgrown the Fostoria plant, it was deemed wise to seek a new location, where could be had all possible advantage for the manufacture and distribution of our wares. . . . Coraopolis, Pa. was selected. . . . The coming season will be the greatest in the history of Lamp making." So the old home of Fostoria Shade and Lamp was abandoned for the new plant in Coraopolis, now under Kopp's able management. By June 10, 1896, Kopp had worked wonders. The Coraopolis plant was featured in a full page article, "The Lamp Makers of America," in CGL. "Mr. Nicholas Kopp, the metal maker and designer, a product of two hemispheres, combining the taste of France with the patient and tireless industry of Germany, topped off with the progressiveness of America, and backed by the enterprise and dash of Mr. Frank Wallace, needs no other encomium than an inspection of the lamps that bear witness to their eminence in their profession and industry. The styles are as varied and diverse as artistic invention, taste, skill, gleaning from all fields, and a study of the best examples of ancient and modern forms could evolve."

The article noted the production of night lamps: "The Dover, Daisy, Sylvan, Acme, Rose and Basket, each and all made in solid opal, turquoise, aqua marine, rose or canary, in glaze or satin finish, decorated in still life scenes, figures, or foliage." The Daisy was the Cosmos (S 286), the Sylvan (S 296) and the Acme (S 383 and 384). The immense size of the factory was applauded: one 15-pot furnace, one six-pot furnace for casing colors, two tanks, ten-pot capacity each, for opal body glass, the factory proper, blowing department, etc. The productive capacity was equal to 31 pots; the glassware made was fine, thin blown and cased glass, outstanding for its artistic shapeliness, beauty of form and grace. An amazing 2,335,200 lamps per year were made, or 800 dozen lamps a day. Besides night lamps, the firm offered banquet lamps and sewing lamps all in the marvelous Kopp colors and decorations.

On July 8, 1896, Kopp again was praised in CGL for his color genius and for his competent staff of 42 artist-decorators to draw landscapes, sea, sky, flowers, and animals on the lamps. Hence the move to Coraopolis meant success and increased sales for Consolidated Lamp, and the company flourished and expanded under the able management of Nicholas Kopp. By 1901, Kopp had left Consolidated to establish his own glass works.

Who was Nicholas Kopp? He was born in Alsace Lorraine in 1865, where his family had been glassmakers for generations. He came to the United States in 1882 to work for Hobbs Glass Company at Wheeling. Like other immigrant glassmakers he moved from plant to plant, staying several years to achieve fame at Consolidated, then going to Swissvale, Pennsylvania, to organize the Kopp Lamp and Glass Company in 1901. This plant merged with Pittsburgh Lamp and Brass and Dithridge and Company in 1902. Kopp became vice president and manager in 1921

The Santa, the Cone and the Columbus lamps in the July 1894 ad by Consolidated

of the new company. He died at the age of 72 on April 16, 1937, according to his obituary in *The New York Times*, April 17, 1937.

A detailed history of both Consolidated Lamp and Glass Company and Nicholas Kopp is essential to the history of the night lamp. More than any other glassmaker, Kopp was responsible for the beauty and variety, the enchanting colorful innovations of the night lamps of 1890-1910. Let us examine now some of the marvelous lamps made at Consolidated. The company produced some of the most precious and durable night lamps: the Kitty Night Lamp, the Iris, the Beacon, the Bristol, the Santa Claus and the Daisy.

Production in the 1890's was brisk. Witness the six night lamps offered in *China, Glass and Lamps*, July 4, 1894: the Santa Claus, the Columbus, the Basket, the No. 2, the No. 800, and the Ermine night lamps. The first two are figural lamps, one a full-figure Santa from Fostoria Shade originally and the other a handsome bust of Columbus (Smith VII and 491, respectively). The next lamps, the Basket (S 279), the No. 2 (S 389), and the No. 800 (S 394) came in rose, turquoise, canary yellow and green. No. 800 or the Cone night lamp in the Cone pattern, was made

S 389, the Basket, and the Ermine lamps in the July 1894 ad by Consolidated

in cased pink or yellow glass or satin glass. The Ermine lamp (S 217) was offered in solid colors in a glossy or a satin finish with a choice of pink, white, turquoise or green. Several lamps were cased with a transparent layer of glass over the colored glass. This gave an exquisite almost two-dimensional effect, unique to Kopp. As we saw earlier, it is probable that all these superb lamps of 1894 were made first by Kopp at Fostoria Shade and Lamp Company prior to the merger with Consolidated.

"The new Sylvan night lamp is a dainty little article and has a big sale already," wrote a critic in CGL, May 30, 1894. The lamp was pictured in an ad the following March 14, 1895, in C & G. An article February 6, 1895, in CGL on "The Glass Trade," called the Sylvan Night Lamp (S 296) a perfect 25¢ night lamp. With its hand painted floral shade and base, the shade as thin and delicate as an eggshell, the lamp was a good buy then and is popular with collectors today.

The Star Night Lamp (S 241) appeared in an article on "The Lamp Makers of America," in CGL, June 10, 1896, and again in the 1902 Consolidated Catalog. In

The Bristol, the Tulip, the Leaf in red satin, and the Beauty by Consolidated

The Sylvan and Star Night Lamps by Consolidated

26

milk glass with a ball shade embossed with cosmos flowers, it had fired-on pink, blue and yellow paint.

The company advertised the Iris night Lamp (S 396) and the Kitty Night Lamp (S 274) February 3, 1898, in C & G. The Iris came in blue satin and in milk glass, while the Kitty lamp was made in painted, embossed milk glass. A year later the Beacon (S 399) appeared. "The Beacon is the latest!" announced the company in an ad in C & G, October 26, 1899. It boasted, too, a large line of decorated all nighters, indicating continued ample production of night lamps. The Beacon (S 399) was decked in brightly colored satin glass, cerise or red, mandarin or orange, and blue.

The Kitty, the Beacon and the Leaf by Consolidated

The Spider Web lamp by Consolidated

The Ray or Rose Night Lamp by Consolidated

Lush wild roses adorned the Duchess (S 303), a dainty milk glass lamp with ball shade and tapered base set on a brass pedestal. With graceful panelling, this lamp came in milk glass and in red satin glass appearing November 1900 in *House Furnisher.* It is pictured here in red satin glass like S 302.

The Plume lamp (S 203) and the Spider Web lamp (S 292) debuted in a Consolidated Lamp and Glass Company Catalog after 1900, seen at the Corning Museum of Glass Library. The latter, found in frosted clear, satin glass and milk glass, was noted for its spider web delicately traced into the glass. The milk glass

The Plume and S 302 by Consolidated

The Daisy or Cosmos in clear and milk glass by Consolidated

Plume lamp had pretty gilt decoration. It has been extensively reproduced in many colors by the L.G. Wright Company. The new lamp is pictured in Chapter XI. The Ray Night Lamp (S 201) also appeared in the post-1900 catalog. Found in milk glass with colorful orange and red fired-on paint, it was an impressive lamp with embossed roses and scrolls. Curiously, Fostoria Glass Company of Moundsville also offered the Plume, the Spider Web and the Ray Night Lamps. Finally, that post-1900 catalog featured the Fairy Night Lamp (S 314 and 313) in painted milk glass with colorful flowers on the ball shade and gracefully tapered base.

Four night lamps by Consolidated were advertised in C & G October 13, 1898: the Paris I and II Night Lamps (S 188, 189); the Daisy or Cosmos lamp (S 286) and No. 2 Night Lamp (S 390). The two Paris lamps were similar, with ribbed panels in the Torquay pattern (Heacock III, 44). While the bases were almost identical, the chimney shades varied somewhat since the shade of the Paris II lamp shown here was fuller than that of Paris I which was oval or egg shaped. Unfortunately, the Paris I lamp was unavailable to photograph. It is pictured in Smith (Fig. 188). Both Paris lamps were milk glass with pink, blue or yellow paint. The Daisy, known to collectors as the Cosmos lamp (S 286), was made in clear, milk glass and cased glass. It is pictured here in clear and milk glass, with pretty painted daisies. Night Lamp 2 (S 390) came in yellow, pink and blue cased glass and was dubbed "The Melon" in an article in HF, October, 1900. It is important to remember that the dates of these ads and articles rarely signify the date the lamp was first made, since all these night lamps were retailed over a 10 year period or longer.

In 1902, Consolidated Lamp published a color catalog boasting "Fine colored glass in rose, canary, and the cerise or red. We now have added the Copper Ruby, which might be better understood as being a dark Mahogany, heretofore manufactured only in Europe." In this catalog were five night lamps: the Tulip in cerise (S 284); the Leaf in cerise or decorated milk glass (S 273); the Beauty in cerise (S 398); the Bristol in decorated milk glass (S 308) and the Star in decorated milk glass (S 241). The three lamps offered in cerise were a striking red satin glass exquisite to behold: the Tulip, Leaf and Beauty Night Lamps. Pictured in color in the center of this book are the following night lamps by Consolidated: the Acme, the Rose, the Cone, the Iris, No. 2 (S 389), the Tulip, the Star, the Daisy or Cosmos, the Kitty and the Leaf.

The Paris II and the Melon by Consolidated

Finally, November 19, 1908 in *Crockery and Glass*, S 374 and S 220 were advertised. S 374 came in pink cased glass and in painted milk glass, while S 220 was made in panelled milk glass with painted violets and in orange satin glass. The night lamps made by Consolidated Lamp and Glass Company were extraordinary, from the delicate designs in milk glass and cased glass to the splendid triumphs in cerise or red satin glass. The creator of these lamps, Nicholas Kopp, was indeed gifted. The beautiful night lamps he developed at Fostoria Shade, Consolidated, and later Pittsburgh mark the apogee in the history of the night lamp.

S 374 and S 220 by Consolidated

The Drape and the Beaded Drape lamps by Pittsburgh

# Chapter IV
# Active Production of Night Lamps

By 1901, Nicholas Kopp had left Consolidated to establish Kopp Lamp and Glass Company in Swissvale, Pennsylvania. In 1902, a consolidation of Pittsburgh Lamp and Brass Company, Dithridge and Company and the Kopp plants occurred. An ad on January 9, 1902, in C & G heralded the merger and announced that the new company, Pittsburgh Lamp, Brass and Glass Company, would make Decorated Opal Novelties, Lead Chimneys, Electrical Glassware, Metal Lamps, Clocks, Mirrors, Onyx Top Tables, Success Lamps, Lamps, Globes, Shades, Colored and Decorated in Kopp Colors. After the merger, the new company produced all the parts of the lamps — the metal fittings, bases, burners, rings at the huge brass department, the glass bodies, feet, chimneys, globes in the glass plants, and the colors and color combinations developed by Kopp in their own laboratory. By June, 1902, each department was working full time to put out the many orders waiting to be filled; business was brisk. Success followed Nicholas Kopp wherever he went! In 1921, he became vice president and general manager of the company. The famous Kopp colors, cardinal red, green, yellow and orange, brought him acclaim at Pittsburgh, too, and beautified the night lamps produced there.

On December 12, 1901, Pittsburgh Lamp and Brass Company offered the Drape night lamp (S 231) and S 272 in *Crockery and Glass.* These lamps continued to be made and sold after the merger in 1902, probably enhanced by Kopp's rich new colors. The Drape lamp came in painted milk glass and in satin glass, while S 272 featured a milk glass ball shade and base in a unique pebbled texture, with embossed, painted daisy and leaf designs. Both the Drape and S 272 are shown in color in the center of this book.

May 29, 1902, in C & G, Pittsburgh offered five night lamps: the Drape (S 231), the Beaded Drape (S 400), S 272, the Tulip (S 285), and S 316. Already the color genius of Nicholas Kopp had manifested itself at Pittsburgh as at Consolidated. These lamps appeared in gorgeous red, green, blue, pink satin glass and in painted and decorated milk glass. Probably Pittsburgh made S 315, 317 and 323, which came from the same mold as S 316, with various decorations either fired-on or painted of pansies, daisies, even praying children as on S 323. The prettiest was the Tulip lamp (S 285) with its brass pedestal and graceful raised tulip petals on its inverted shade and base, in red, blue and green satin glass, shown in color in the middle of this book with the Beaded Drape. Kopp surpassed all competitors with his brilliantly colored satin glass night lamps.

S 316, 323, 272 and The Tulip (S 285) by Pittsburgh

The Nellie Bly by Dithridge and Pittsburgh

Pittsburgh promoted the famous Nellie Bly lamp (S 219), originally a Dithridge lamp, with its daisy decked base and frosted pearl top shade, and also a tiny lamp resembling a bamboo basket, possibly S 277 in C & G, April 21, 1904. By May 25, 1911, the same journal reported that the company showed their most extensive line of night lamps, with 15 new designs in a hundred different treatments. On June 8, 1911, *Crockery and Glass Journal* noted that Pittsburgh had 22 different styles of night lamps, all with matching shades in various colors and decorations. Even as late as 1915, the company featured oil lamps in many new designs, plain and decorated in Kopp's colors. Demand for oil lamps continued, particularly in sections of the country without gas and electricity, according to C & G, September 16, 1915.

Few photo ads exist showing Pittsburgh Lamp, Brass and Glass Company's night lamps. Articles provide more information than do the ads. Collectors might note that the company's Beaded Drape lamp (S 400) has been extensively reproduced by the L.G. Wright Company in both milk glass and satin glass. More information on this is in Chapter XI.

Dithridge and Company of Pittsburgh, Pennsylvania, was an old, established glass company dating back to 1860. Active in lamp production from 1881, the firm patented several designs for lamps, chimneys and lampshades, according to A.C. Revi in *American Pressed Glass and Figural Bottles*.

Before it became part of the Pittsburgh Lamp, Brass and Glass Company, Dithridge produced several night lamps. October 28, 1891, in CGL, they presented the Baby Cleveland Night Lamp (S 218) which came in milk glass with various decorations. The Mother Goose Night Lamp (S 186) debuted February 24, 1892, in CGL and was called "Our Latest Idea", "A Taking Easter Novelty." It came in three colors with three different decorations of flowers. Indeed, this tiny lamp with its egg-shaped base and matching chimney shade must have delighted children on Easter morning. Perhaps it came in an Easter basket along with candies and glass eggs. The Sylvia Banquet Lamp (S 326) appeared in CGL, December 13, 1893. Almost 15" high, it was a milk glass peg lamp that fit into a tall matching candlestick. Painted with flowers, leaves and angels, it had a chimney shade almost exactly like the Nellie Bly shade. All three of these lamps appear in color in the center of this book.

The Mother Goose, Baby Cleveland and Sylvia lamps by Dithridge

Dalzell's Sweetheart Lamp

On October 3, 1894, a critic in CGL noted that Dithridge had produced several fine night lamps: No. 500, No. 800, Nellie Bly, Esther, Sylvia and Princess. As we have seen, the Sylvia was a miniature banquet lamp. Unfortunately, none of these lamps was pictured. We can deduce, however, from this article that Dithridge made the Nellie Bly lamp (S 219) and also from the patent illustration of March 25, 1890, pictured in *American Pressed Glass*, p. 136. Revi shows a design for a pressed and blown lamp that is identical to the Nellie Bly lamp. Made to commemorate Nellie Bly's trip around the world, the lamp sold very well.

Who was Nellie Bly? She was an American journalist who worked for *The Pittsburgh Dispatch* and *The New York World*. In 1889, she went around the world in less than 80 days, beginning her trip November 14 in New York and completing it there by January 25, 1890. Trying to beat the record of Jules Verne's Phineas Fogg, she circled the world in 72 days. This trip received much publicity and marked the zenith of her career. The Nellie Bly lamp commemorated her feat and was a fine tribute to a modern woman! After the merger, Pittsburgh Lamp, Brass and Glass re-offered the Nellie Bly lamp in 1904.

The Teardrop with Eyewinker and Crown lamps by Dalzell

Like Nicholas Kopp, W.A.B. Dalzell was an eminent glassmaker. In 1884, he established Dalzell Brothers and Gilmore in Wellsville, West Virginia, and in 1888 the plant moved to Findlay, Ohio, and was renamed Dalzell, Gilmore and Leighton. In 1901, after selling out to the National Glass Company, he became vice president and later president of Fostoria Glass. Dalzell stayed with Fostoria from 1901 until his death in 1928 and became one of the best glass producers in the country, according to his obituary in PGBS, March 15, 1928.

Dalzell, Gilmore and Leighton in Findlay, Ohio, had a brief but magnificent period of lamp production before they were absorbed into the National Glass Company on November 22, 1899. Don Smith in *Findlay Pattern Glass* recounts their history. The company developed a machine to manufacture kerosene lamps in which the oil font and lamp stem were one piece made in the same mold. Previously, many lamps had been hand-made, with the stem pressed in one mold and the font blown in another. They also invented the clinch collar, which was attached to the lamp while the glass was still soft. The National Glass Company acquired the patent to the clinch collar and to the lamp mold machines. Famous Dalzell patterns included the Sweetheart, Priscilla, Eyewinker, Columbia and Crown. Kerosene lamps were their main product from 1899 to 1901, and 50,000 dozen lamps were sold in one season, 1898-99.

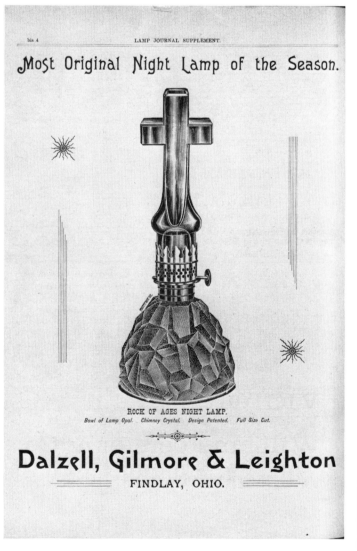

The Dakota Night Lamp
CGL May 2, 1901
Reproduced from the collection of the Library of Congress

The Rock of Ages Night Lamp
PGR June 2, 1892.
Reproduced from the collection of the Library of Congress

Which night lamps did Dalzell, Gilmore, and Leighton make? The famous Sweetheart lamp (S 109), also called the Beaded Heart, was their product and came in large and small sizes. These lamps were made in combinations of green and clear glass, and some had frosted hearts and hand-painted flowers, according to the ad in *Illustrated Glass and Pottery World,* August, 1898. The company also produced the Teardrop with Eyewinker (S 115) in large and small lamps as well as the Crown lamp (S 108), advertised in November, 1897, in the same journal.

Shown here is a full-page ad by the National Glass Company, operating Dalzell Gilmore and Leighton, as it appeared May 2, 1901, in *China, Glass and Lamps.* It pictured the Dakota Night Lamp, a clear glass lamp with a tripod pedestal and raised fleur-de-lis on the panels at the top and bottom of the lamp.

One of the most uncommon night lamps ever made was offered by the Dalzell company, June 2, 1892, in PGR. The Rock of Ages Night Lamp had a milk glass base fashioned like a craggy rock with a clear chimney shaped like a cross. Advertised as the "Most Original Night Lamp of the Season," this lamp would thrill the modern collector, but one has never been found. The ad is reprinted here.

Perry McDonald with the Ferns and Flowers night lamp S 282

Nail City Stamping Company of Wheeling, West Virginia, offered four handsome night lamps in the 1890's. Three were introduced in C & G, July 6, 1893: S 281, S 282, and S 54. With shade and base resembling a scallop shell, the Shell lamp (S 281) came in a white glossy finish and in milk glass, both stippled in gold, blue and crimson with a very wide 6" diameter shade. Its mate, S 282, appeared in two styles: milk glass, ivory or turquoise with a glossy finish, and in a white matt finish stippled in gold, blue and crimson. The S 282 was in the Ferns and Flowers pattern (Heacock III, p. 24).

The tiny milk glass hand lamp, S 54, had a solid brass band around its middle and came in milk glass, ivory and turquoise. A year later, July 26, 1894, in C & G, the company offered a milk glass lamp with a ball shade decorated with a dainty angel on tiptoe picking flowers from a garden (S 324). Nail City Stamping Company called itself, Manufacturers of Lamps, Lanterns, Oil Cans and Specialties and made a welcome contribution to the history of the night lamp with its bold, innovative lamps.

S 54, the Ferns & Flowers (S 282), the Shell (S 281) and S 324 by Nail City

The Stars and Bars lamp by Bellaire Goblet with the new lamp by Wright

S 118 and S 477 by Bellaire Goblet

Articles and ads in C & G from 1893 to 1897 indicate the Nail City Stamping Company was purchased by Wheeling Stamping Company in 1897. By June 24, 1897, Wheeling had completed the merger and taken over management of the Nail City plant. Shortly thereafter, on September 2, 1897, an ad appeared for Wheeling Stamping, successors to Nail City Stamping, promoting and listing their products. Night lamps were not mentioned. It is probable that night lamps were not offered after the merger. Hence, the period of night lamp production by Nail City was brief, 1893-1894, making these lamps more scarce and valuable today.

The Bellaire Goblet Company of Findlay and Bellaire, Ohio, made some night lamps S 118, 477, 482 and a Saucer Base lamp. *Lamps and Other Lighting Devices 1850-1906,* on pp. 96-97, shows plates from Bellaire's 1891 catalog with three of these lamps pictured, S 118, S 477 and the Saucer Base lamp.

Bellaire Goblet merged with the U.S. Glass Company in 1891, and subsequently U.S. Glass offered all these night lamps. The Saucer Base and the Stars and Bars lamps appeared in the large color USGC catalog, reprinted in Thuro, pp. 326-327. Prior to this, on November 18, 1886, in C & G, Bellaire Goblet advertised the Stars and Bars lamp (S 482) and its mate the Stars and Bars Cigar Lighter lamp. The latter had an inverted shade like its twin, but its base was barrel-shaped and surrounded by at least three cigar lighters with diamond shaped tips. All these lamps came in blue, amber and crystal. The Stars and Bars lamp was reproduced recently by the L.G. Wright Company, as discussed in Chapter XI. Night lamp production continued to be very active from 1890 to 1910, with superb lamps produced by Dithridge, Pittsburgh, Dalzell, Nail City and Bellaire Goblet.

S 211 and the Juno by Eagle Glass

The Eagle, S 200, S 445 by Eagle Glass

# Chapter V
# Eagle, Fostoria and Gillinder

Competition was sharp and interest immense in the tiny night lamps. What new colors, shapes, designs could the companies devise next, customers wondered? Truly, the variety must have delighted the hearts of those Victorian ladies with their love for ornament and decoration. Eagle Glass Company, Fostoria and Gillinder were all active in night lamp production.

Eagle Glass Company of Wellsburg, West Virginia, exhibited night lamps at several large glass exhibitions in Pittsburgh, from 1899 to 1912, at the Monongahela House, the regional center for trade fairs and exhibits with sales-rooms for wholesalers. Often these lamps had matching salt and pepper shakers, and the base to the salt was also the base of the lamp. These night lamps were popular and sold well. In January, 1907, the company displayed a varied collection of night lamps, many with Art Nouveau decorations and shapes. Certainly S 200 had the lush swirling plumes common to Art Nouveau design. The Jewel Night Lamp was made to rest on a small plate which caught drips and held matches, perhaps S 35. The 1907 exhibit was the largest and most complete showing of night lamps by an American firm, according to C & G, January 12, 1907. In January, 1909, at the Monongahela House the company took three rooms and showed another large array of night lamps, Easter novelties, salts, peppers in plain and decorated milk glass, reported C & G.

Eagle Glass presented the Juno Night Lamp (S 214) in plain milk glass or milk glass painted crimson, gold or green with an embossed Maltese Cross design in a full page ad in *China Glass and Lamps* July 22, 1896. The following year, they advertised S 210 made from the same mold as the Juno, but decorated with painted birds, flowers, a house and a bridge instead of the Maltese Cross. The lamp was pictured in an ad in C & G in December, 1897. Since S 211 is almost identical in shape and design to the Juno, we can assume Eagle Glass made it, too.

In 1898 appeared their most famous milk glass lamp, the Eagle Night Lamp (S 275). With an embossed eagle on its blue and yellow base and ball shade it was advertised in CGL, June 29, 1898. The following May 18 in C & G, Eagle featured S 200 and its twin S 445 lamps in milk glass and amber glass, respectively. On June 29, 1899, Eagle offered S 223 in milk glass with gilt decoration, S 200, and 214 in C & G. Pictured in color in the center of this book are four lamps by Eagle: the Juno (S 214), S 200, the Fleur-de-Lis (S 228) and the Eagle (S 275).

Eagle Glass Company promoted the Fleur-de-Lis lamp (S 228) October 10, 1901, in CGL. It came in clear and milk glass with the large fleur-de-lis painted red, gold or black. This lamp is reproduced today in pale green and cobalt blue, colors it never came in originally, and is discussed in Chapter XI.

Finally, Eagle produced a dainty milk glass night lamp  S 173 with matching salt and pepper shakers, advertised January 14, 1904, in C & G. From the Juno to the Eagle to the Fleur-de-Lis, Eagle Glass had an exciting line of night lamps. Unfortunately, their ads rarely featured illustrations of their lamps. We can assume that they made hundreds of night lamps and specialized in those with matching salts and peppers.

Fostoria Glass Company began production in Fostoria, Ohio, in 1887, with Lucien B. Martin as the company's first president. In 1891, Fostoria Glass moved to Moundsville, West Virginia, where from 1901-1928 it was under the able management of W.A.B. Dalzell.

Fostoria made table lamps as well as night lamps and began to produce the latter in 1890. The Annie Rooney Night Lamp was presented in July, 1890. By August 30, 1900, a critic for C & G wrote: "The Fostoria Glass Co. have won fame for their lines of lamps and flint glass all over this continent. Not only are their shapes and designs excellent, but their reputation for good workmanship and quality of material is widespread." The Fostoria artists were adept at painting realistic flowers on the lamp shades and bases.

The Fostoria catalogs depicted some night lamps such as the Kenova, the Rose and the Dixie in patterned milk glass with ball or chimney shades. One catalog, circa 1900, which belongs to William Heacock showed six night lamps: the Princess (S 203), the Robin Hood (S 292), the Bohemia Boudoir (S 307), the Texas (S 201), No. 5 or S 184 and the Dixie. The Texas was better known as the Rose Night Lamp. The Dixie featured a milk glass base and chimney shade with large embossed painted plumes. Courtesy of Mr. Heacock, the page of night lamps from the catalog appears here. Also pictured are five of these same lamps as they look today, with three of them, the Dixie, the Texas and the Plume lamps shown in color in the center of this book.

Fostoria presented the Annie Rooney Night Lamp (S 148) on July 10, 1890, in PGR. It came in clear or clear and frosted glass. We can assume that the company also made S 151, as it is nearly identical to the Annie Rooney and both feature the

S 173 and the Fleur-de-Lis by Eagle

# NIGHT LAMPS

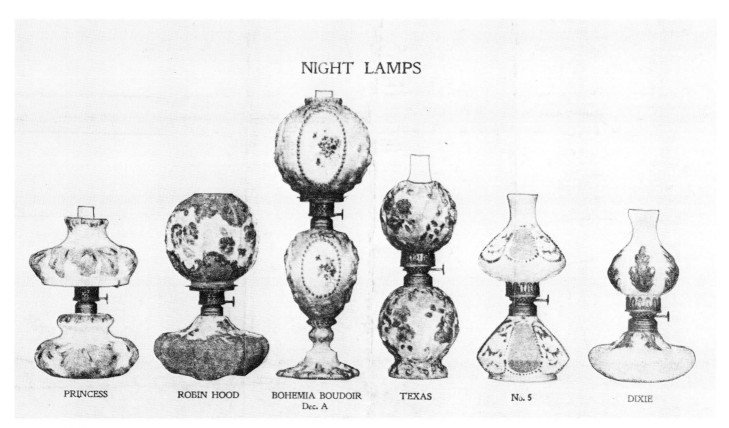

PRINCESS     ROBIN HOOD     BOHEMIA BOUDOIR     TEXAS     No. 5     DIXIE
                                 Dec. A

Fostoria Night Lamps from the Fostoria Catalog

The Princess or Plume, the Robin Hood or Spider Web lamp, the Texas or Rose lamp, No. 5 and the Dixie by Fostoria

45

famous Virginia pattern (Kamm V, 139). In a Fostoria Catalog No. 4, circa 1890, was the tiny milk glass Kenova Night Lamp (S 197) which had large oak leaves embossed and painted on the base.

A July 20, 1898, ad in CGL pictured three Fostoria lamps: S 184, S 57 and a milk glass lamp base with a beaded rim and an embossed stylized rising sun. The Robin Hood Night Lamp (S 292) with embossed pansies and a delicate spider web traced in the glass appeared August 9, 1900, on the front page of *Crockery and Glass,* and also in the catalogs. That same month in that journal, the Rose Night Lamp (S 201) was pictured as one of the latest products of Fostoria Glass. In 1906, it was offered again in a Fostoria catalog with the Clover Night Lamp and Night Lamp 1112. The reprint from this catalog is found in *Lamps and Other Lighting Devices,* pp. 151 and 154. The Clover Night Lamp (S 133) came in clear or clear glass painted red, with a diamond pattern punctuated by flowers. No. 1112 Night Lamp, or S 132,

Fostoria's Annie Rooney Night Lamp

The Kenova, S 184, S 57 of Fostoria

S 132 and the Clover Night Lamp of Fostoria Glass

The Bead and Panel night lamp by Fostoria Glass

S 320 by Fostoria Glass

was made in clear or painted glass, too. Most of the color has worn off these lamps today. In that same 1906 catalog was a No. 19 Night Lamp in blue or clear glass with a fluted chimney and a panelled base with a beaded drape in each panel, called the Bead and Panel night lamp.

In my collection is a bisque-finish opaline lamp, like S 320, painted green with red roses on the base and shade with fringe around the shade. Undoubtedly Fostoria made this and also S 321 and 322. This fringed lamp appears in color on the dressing table in the middle of this book. The decoration on these lamps was carefully hand-painted by skilled artists and was superior to the art work on other night lamps. Attribution for the lamp derives from a picture of a similar full-sized table lamp with a fringed shade in *Crockery and Glass,* April 22, 1915. Comparing the night lamp to this full-sized lamp, we note these similarities: the shades are identical in shape and decoration; both have dark shading at the top of their umbrella shades and hand-painted roses at the bottom with ample fringe attached to the base of the shade. On the lamp base, the dark shading yields to lovely hand-painted pastel roses. The shapes of the bases differ in that the table lamp has a brass pedestal. Since few other companies made lamps with hand-painted, fringed shades, we can conclude that Fostoria made Fig. 320, 321, 322.

Induction also leads to the conclusion that Fostoria made S 266, a lovely milk glass lamp with an umbrella shade and an embossed inverted heart-shape design around the lower part of the shade and base. William Heacock pictures a syrup in Book III, 60 which is identical in pattern to S 266. The syrup is from a Fostoria Glass Company Catalog. As the patterns are identical, we can assume that Fostoria also made the night lamp S 266.

As was explained in Chapter III, Fostoria Glass Company and Consolidated offered the identical lamps, S 201, S 203 and S 292. Fostoria called S 201 the Rose Night Lamp in a catalog of 1906, while Consolidated dubbed its lamp the Ray Night Lamp in a post-1900 catalog. The Plume lamp (S 203) was in this catalog and in Fostoria's catalog circa 1900, where it was called The Princess. The lamp which collectors call the Spider Web lamp (S 292) was Fostoria's Robin Hood Lamp in the 1900 catalog, while the same lamp, called No. 9, appeared in the post-1900 Consolidated catalog. What explains this duplication? The lax enforcement of patents by the U.S. Patent Office, the presence of both these companies in Fostoria, Ohio, in the early 1890s and the migration of glass designers and workers from one factory to another might account for the duplication.

In 1859, the U.S. Patent Office was established, but it was only in 1892 that the patent and copyright drawings of the designs were required. Before then, the designs were registered with a number and the name of the firm, with no portrayal of the design. Often the original designers of a patent didn't care if it were copied, Minnie Kamm points out in the Introduction to Books IV and V. She notes that design and mold makers were paid large amounts of money and that a glass firm could attain a high rank by the perfection and superiority of its designs. Gillinder, Duncan, LaBelle and Northwood made the best patterns. Many of the designers of glassware hailed from Europe and were true artists; the best designers migrated from plant to plant. This migration and the casual attitude of the Patent Office explain why two companies could offer the same night lamp as in the case of the Rose, the Plume and the Spider Web lamps.

Founded in 1861 in Philadelphia, Pennsylvania, Gillinder and Sons made lighting glassware, pressed and cut tableware, window glass and druggist glassware. At the 1876 Centennial Exhibition in Philadelphia, they set up an

S 266 of Fostoria Glass

Satin Glass Gillinder lamps: Pearl Baby McKee, Baby McKee and S 395

Earliest Gillinder lamps: the Westmoreland and the Baby McKee

exhibition factory where centennial souvenirs such as little glass slippers, statues and paperweights were signed and sold. Here, too, they saw on exhibit the fine satin glass from France and decided to duplicate it, Kamm notes in Book VI. By 1879, the company was one of the largest firms in the country with 325 employees.

Gillinder produced several splendid night lamps. Two early ones were made in satin glass: the Baby McKee and the Pearl Baby McKee Night Lamps (S 393 and S 299). In decorated white satin, Baby McKee was born October 3, 1889, followed by Pearl Baby McKee January 16, 1890, in PGR. Made in white, green and blue ribbed satin glass, the Pearl Baby McKee was called the neatest and cutest night lamp made. Gillinder also produced S 300 and S 301 which resembled the Pearl Baby McKee, but added painted floral decorations and silver overlay, respectively. The Baby McKee Night Lamps sold very well and were praised at the 1891 Monongahela House Exhibit in Pittsburgh. One critic wrote in PGR, October 1, 1891: "The small night lamps made by this firm in colored bisque glass with shades to match, have no rivals for a light suitable for bedroom or sick chamber, a sufficient light being given with very little heat or consumption of oil. They are made in two shapes and a number of colors and decorations." By 1892, Gillinder night lamps were very popular and comprised colored and decorated milk glass in 20 shapes and patterns, according to PGR, October 20, 1892.

The Westmoreland Night Lamp (S 144) was offered in an ad in PGR, January 16, 1890. The Westmoreland pattern, a collection of diamond shapes in clear pressed glass, was first made in 1889-1890. Coming in 75 pieces including a punch bowl, it sold very well, Kamm notes in Book II. Indeed, the night lamp sparkles as if with myriad gems. It has an umbrella shade and an oddly molded base, since mold lines bisect it like a cross at its mid section. Gillinder also made S 145 and 146, both in the popular Westmoreland pattern.

Two years later, on October 27, 1892, in PGR, appeared another beautiful night lamp S 395 which came in milk glass or blue satin glass as shown here with myriad embossed daisies. The Defender (S 240) was introduced November 6, 1895, in CGL, in turquoise, green, and white milk glass, sometimes decorated with painted flowers between the stylized leaves. "The Queen 'Tis a Beauty You Should Have it," heralded The Queen (S 236), a delicate scroll-embossed milk glass lamp

Gillinder's Three Westmoreland Lamps: S 144, 146, 145

The Defender and the Queen by Gillinder

with a ball shade and a base graced with painted spring flowers. It was also offered in the same colors as the Defender, in CGL, August 18, 1897. In color, this lamp is the same as S 234. Uncle Sam's Night Lamp (S 310 and S 311) appeared August 17, 1898, in CGL. It was pictured in white milk glass decorated with violets, and also came in glossy turquoise, green as shown here, or white.

One of the most unusual Gillinder lamps was The Primrose, debuting in CGL, September 30, 1896. Made in turquoise, Nile green and white, it had an embossed basket on the base and shade. In the basket were bouquets of primroses and daisies. The glass is an exquisite glossy smooth milk glass. What good fortune it was to find this green lamp in the collection of Helen Feltner, who allowed me to carry it home and photograph it on the dressing table in a color photo in the center of this book. Also in color are S 240, S 293, S 236, the Primrose and S 310.

I have several Gillinder lamps in my collection and enjoy them for their beauty, rarity, design and quality. A critic wrote October 20, 1897, in CGL: "The Gillinder glass has long had a national reputation. It is highly favored by retailers as well as among housekeepers. It sells well, has a brilliant appearance and is marked at low rates." Gillinder made some of the earliest, prettiest night lamps marketed on a large scale. In 1961, the company celebrated 100 years in the glass business. With its competitors Eagle Glass and Fostoria Glass, Gillinder added beauty and grace to the night lamps at the turn of the century.

The Primrose and Uncle Sam's Night Lamp by Gillinder

Two Acme and Three Rose lamps
by Consolidated

The Star, the Daisy, the Kitty and the Leaf
by Consolidated

The Cone, the Iris, S 389 and the Tulip
by Consolidated

S 272, the Drape, the Beaded Drape and the Tulip by Pittsburgh Lamp, Brass & Glass

The Mother Goose, Baby Cleveland and Sylvia lamps by Dithridge

The Juno, S 200, the Fleur-de-Lis and the Eagle by Eagle Glass

The Dixie, the Rose and the Plume by Fostoria Glass

Defender, the Baby McKee, the Queen, the Primrose and the Uncle Sam's Night Lamp by Gillinder

Victorian Dressing Table with S 320 of Fostoria Glass and The Primrose by Gillinder

The Plain Windows and Opalescent Swirl lamps by Hobbs Glass

The Bounty by Pairpoint Glass

The New Art Night Lamp in cranberry and End-of-Day Glass, the Little Beauty and the Twinkle by Noe

The Stars and Bars, the Match-holder, the Remington and the Swirl lamps by U.S. Glass

The old and new Daisy and Button with Thumbprint lamps, the Star and Panel by A.A. Importing and the amber Plume lamp by Wright.

The Boutique lamps by Imperial on both ends, two new Fleur-de-Lis lamps, the new green Bundling lamp by Imperial and the old Imperial No. 9 lamp

The Handy Night Lamp

The Noxall Night Lamp

# Chapter VI
# William R. Noe

One of the most amazing entrepreneurs in the lamp business was William Noe, who astonished the trade in 1900 with his line of 10-cent night lamps. "How it is possible to turn out as big a lamp as well made and nicely finished, complete with wick, chimney and burner, at a price which will enable a dealer to sell it for a dime at retail, is puzzling a good many people," exclaimed *The Crockery and Glass Journal* September 27, 1900. Who was William Noe and how could he afford to sell night lamps so cheaply? He was a jobber or wholesale dealer in lamps, an importer of lighting devices with a New York and Hamburg, Germany address. Probably he imported many of his 10-cent goods from Germany, including the Little Beauty Night Lamp (S 439) which he claimed was the most popular night lamp ever offered.

Noe was not only an importer, but also a manufacturer. In 1895, he manufactured the primitive Handy Night Lamp (S 4) with its reflector and raised metal burner, and offered it for five cents! Today, it sells for $45.00. Active in the lamp trade from 1895 to 1920, Noe owned a brass goods factory in Brooklyn and a large lamp, shade and novelty factory in New York.

Among the goods Noe retailed for a dime in 1900 was the Twinkle Lamp, so popular with collectors today. He also marketed small tin lamps at 10 cents each. Colored glass, satin glass and cased glass lamps all were either imported or made by Noe. From 1895 or perhaps earlier, until his sudden death in 1920, Noe was a dramatic force in the development of the night lamp. We can thank him for the Little Buttercup, the Twinkle, the Handy and the Comet lamps. He was one of the largest producers and most reasonable wholesalers in the trade, as well as a man with a dramatic flair and considerable skill in merchandising.

Beginning in 1895 with the Handy Lamp (S 4), Noe entered the market aggressively and his lamps sold very well, according to CGL, May 29, 1895. Identical to the Handy Lamp was the All Night Lamp, with the name "All Night Lamp Co. N.Y." embossed on the clear font. Advertised October 24, 1895, in C & G, it had a metal burner and reflector like the Handy Lamp. The following year, May 21, 1896, in C & G, Noe presented the Dresden, which featured a baby lying on its back to form the bottom of the lamp, with the lamp base cradled on the baby's stomach. This bizarre imported lamp had a milk glass umbrella shade and a painted bisque-finish base. It was unavailable to photograph. A year later in the same journal, November 11, 1897, appeared the Noxall Night Lamp (S 22) in clear glass with a sheaf of wheat and its name embossed on the base. With its white beehive shade, this lamp retailed for a dime.

The Little Beauty Night Lamp (S 439) was introduced on October 12, 1899 in C &G in an ad that showed a little girl in a long night dress lighting her night light. Selling for $2.00 a dozen, the lamp was imported and came in three shapes and six different colors, such as pink, red, green and amberina. A year later, September 27, 1900, in the same journal, The Twinkle (S 432) appeared as one of Noe's lamps that could be sold for a dime. It came in purple, green, amber and blue glass. Several painted tin lamps were in that same ad, including one with little bees and hives called "The Hummer." A critic wrote February 1, 1912, in C & G, that Noe had "a sort of curiosity shop in lighting devices. . . . The specialties in miniature lamps are particularly interesting." The most majestic of Noe's lamps was The Empress (S 601), a true art glass lamp in pink, blue, yellow, green and white mother of pearl satin glass, introduced in HF, October, 1900.

The New Beauty Night Lamp (S 367) was advertised in December, 1900, in *House Furnisher* and was probably imported. A rather large 9" high lamp, it came in End-of-Day glass, ruby, amberina, purple and green in a Beaded Rib pattern. It was unavailable to photograph, but resembles The New Art Night Lamp (S 369) pictured here.

One of the most elegant imports from Germany was the Vienna Night Lamp (S 386). Produced in pink, cherry, green, yellow and blue cased glass, it was decorated with a raised gold floral spray on the base and ball shade. *House Furnisher* claimed in August, 1901, that "The lamps with their shades . . . are just the thing for a dressing table." Depending on high volume, Noe sold his lamps at very low prices; for example, the Vienna was $21.00 a dozen.

The Little Buttercup Lamp (S 36) was presented by Noe on December 1, 1904, in C & G. Collectors delight in this colorful glass lamp with its applied handle and embossed title, and try to find it in an array of colors: clear, amber, amethyst, green and cobalt. Colorful lamps were a specialty of William Noe. Witness the End-of-Day glass lamp offered January 19, 1905, in C & G. Called the New Art Night Lamp (S 369) it was his second End-of-Day glass lamp, almost identical to the New Beauty (S 367), but the New Art had a Beaded Swirl pattern. It came not only in End-of-Day glass, but also in green, clear, cranberry, amethyst and milk glass. It is pictured in the center of the book in color in cranberry and End-of-Day glass with the Little Beauty and the Twinkle lamps.

The Little Beauty (S 439) and The Twinkle (S 432) Night Lamps

The New Art Night Lamp in cranberry and End-of-Day glass

The Little Buttercup

The Vienna and the Empress night lamps

Noe advertised the Comet lamp (S 78) in C & G, November 4, 1920, the year of his death. Undoubtedly made to compete with Silver and Company's Little Beauty Night Lamp (S 77), the Comet was also a miniature hanging lamp. An article November 4, 1920, in C & G, recommended it to light the home after the family had retired, claimed it could burn several nights without needing fuel and boasted it had no odor, smoke or soot. Producing a soft glow, it did not need a daily cleaning. It was made in solid brass with a brass or nickel finish, and hung in the hallway outside the bedrooms or in the bathroom. Collectors today hang the Comet in their bathrooms.

Manufacturer, importer, lamp dynamo, William Noe won acclaim for his bargain prices, his clever ads and for the flamboyant way he brought the lovely German night lamps and his own colorful lamps into the thriving American market. "Good for Any Night, All Night and All Right" (C & G, October 24, 1895).

The Comet

# Chapter VII
# Metal Night Lamps

While Plume and Atwood was the most prominent producer of metal night lamps, they were made also by Edward Miller and Company, Silver and Company, the Vapo-Cresolene Company, the Rochester Lamp Company, and others. The Plume and Atwood Manufacturing Company made burners for lamps and also handsome brass and nickel night lamps. The Nutmeg and the Cottage night lamps were offered as early as 1881. The Nutmeg came in clear and colored glass with a tiny metal handle, while the Cottage was produced in brass or nickel with a saucer base, a perfect chamber lamp. Most metal lamps were either brass or nickel plated. Polished, they look gorgeous hanging in a bathroom or sitting on a kitchen shelf.

As early as May 3, 1877, P and A offered in *Crockery and Glass Journal* the Little Banner Night Lamp, a small flat, disc-shaped crystal lamp with a series of embossed dots around its circumference and a tiny opal chimney. Standing only 4½″ high to the top of its chimney, it resembled the early kerosene lamps of L.H. Olmstead and Nicholas Wapler, discussed in Chapter II. It evolved later into the Improved Banner Lamp. Both these and the Nutmeg lamps were glass lamps, but since they were P & A products they belong in this chapter.

The Plume and Atwood Company offered the Cottage, the Little Duchess (S 32), the Nutmeg (S 29), the Improved Banner (S 20) in PGR on October 6, 1881, and again on April 22, 1886. The Nutmeg, a glass lamp with a metal band around its circumference, came in myriad colors: green, cobalt blue, milk glass and clear, the last two shown here. The Little Duchess (S 32) was offered in milk glass and blue glass, with the embossed words "Little Duchess" on the font and a brass saucer base. Similarly, the Improved Banner had its name embossed on the font with three stars, like the Little Duchess and the Nutmeg, and was made in clear and milk glass with an Olmstead type burner.

In *The Plume and Atwood Manufacturing Company Catalog* circa 1906, reprinted and given to me to reproduce here by J.W. Courter, was a page of Bedroom Night Lamps including the Nutmeg, Cottage, Acorn, Little Brownie (S 59), Hornet and Fireside. Also pictured in this catalog was The Little Royal Lamp (S 92), which came as a standing lamp shown here and also as a bracket, hand and harp lamp. Both it and the five metal Bedroom Night Lamps were made in brass or nickel. The Fireside and the Little Brownie had metal reflectors and

The Little Banner by P & A

Two Improved Banner lamps, the Little Duchess and the Little Brownie by P & A

# Bedroom Night Lamps

The Nutmeg lamps in milk glass and clear glass by P & A

**No. 181. Nutmeg.**
7 ins. high.
Glass Bowl, Wire Handle.
No. 1516 Nutmeg Burner.

**No. 182. Cottage.**
6¾ ins. high.
All Metal.
No. 1516 Nutmeg Burner.

**No. 2127. Acorn.**
5¼ ins. high.
All Metal.
No. 733 Acorn Burner.

**All** above take Nutmeg Chimney and Wick.

No. 181 Lamp is packed regular in assorted colors, Flint, Opal and Blue.

**No. 1290. Little Brownie.**
7½ ins. high.
All Metal.
No. 663 Hornet Burner.
Takes Hornet
Chimney and Wick.

**No. 739. Hornet.**
7¾ ins. high.
All Metal.
No. 663 Hornet Burner.
Takes Hornet
Chimney and Wick.

**No. 2130. Fireside.**
6½ ins. high.
All Metal.
No. 1516 Nutmeg Burner
Takes Nutmeg
Chimney and Wick.

The Acorn lamp of P & A

Reprinted from the Plume and Atwood Manufacturing Company Catalog

The Little Royal Lamp of P & A

hooks for hanging. As was noted earlier, trade journal ads indicated that these lamps were made several years before 1906. They must have proved popular and endured some modification in styles. The Cottage and Fireside lamps were pictured by Dean Langness from his collection.

Besides a plethora of metal lamps, the P & A Company made night lamp burners, such as the Acorn, the Nutmeg and the Hornet, at 95¢ to $1.10 a dozen, as well as other metal parts for small lamps. For more than half a century, P & A produced kerosene lamps and lamp parts.

Edward Miller and Company of Meriden, Connecticut, signed many of their metal night lamps "E.M. and Company". A saucer base lamp (S 31) with nickel plated or brass finish was signed, as was the nickel plated Acme lamp (S 64).

The Acme lamp S 64 by E. Miller

The Cottage and the Fireside by P & A

Another nickel lamp, with the embossed words "All Night" on the top rim, was marked E.M. on the burner. Shown here on the left, it lacks part of the burner and the reflector. The Midget, a small metal hand lamp pictured here with an embossed floral handle and tiny burner cap, was marked "E. Miller and Company" on the burner and "Made in the United States of America" on the base. Perhaps some collectors have other night lamps signed "E.M." on the base or burner and can now properly identify their lamps.

The Little Beauty Night Lamp (S 77), patented in 1889, was offered by Silver and Company, Brooklyn, for a number of years. *The Housewife* of August, 1891 pictured it at 50¢, or as a premium for anyone who brought in new subscribers to the magazine. It was made of nickel plated brass and could burn 30 hours. Almost 25 years later, June 24, 1915, it appeared again in a Silver and Company ad in C & G.

The Midget by Miller and Co.

The All Night Lamp and S 31 of Edward Miller and Co.

The Little Beauty Night Lamp of Silver and Company

This is one of the few trade journal ads where the lamp was shown in actual use, hanging in the bathroom, the bedroom, the hall and the kitchen. The lamp was usually signed "Silver and Company" on the back. The ad called it the largest selling night lamp in the world.

The Vapo-Cresolene lamp (S 630) appeared in a December, 1892 ad in *The Housewife* as "A Specific for Whooping Cough". Pictured with vaporizer fumes rising from the tiny pan on top of the lamp, it claimed to be a disinfectant, an antiseptic, a cure for whooping cough, a remedy for asthma, catarrh, colds, diphtheria, croup, yellow fever, hay fever and sore throat. The lamp was patented in 1885, and was made by the Vapo-Cresolene Company of New York. Selling for $1.75 for the lamp and the vaporizer liquid trade-named Cresolene, the lamp had directions for use on the box: "Fill the lamp with the best Kerosene Oil obtainable. . . . Light the lamp allowing as large a flame as possible; but care must be taken for the first 15 minutes to see that it does not smoke. Place the lamp under the Vaporizer. Place the Vaporizer in a tin or crockery dish to guard against overturning, and set the dish on a table near the bed, but out of reach of small children. Lastly fill the movable saucer with Cresolene." Cresolene was put in the saucer on top of the lamp and used to relieve congestion.

Swirl Vaporizer lamp and the Vapo-Cresolene lamp

The Vapo-Cresolene lamp was sold for a number of years until the FDA withdrew it from the market for false claims in 1930. Apparently the foul-smelling Cresolene did not vindicate its claim to destroy all germs. Sometimes the lamp is found in the original box complete with the bottle of Cresolene as illustrated here.

Recently, I discovered another vaporizer lamp at an antiques show and bought it. In a wire cage with a vaporizer tray like the Vapo-Cresolene, the lamp had a clear glass swirl base, a screw-on burner and a chimney with a ring around the bottom and the words Pyrex Y M. The swirl lamp was 4½" high to the top of the chimney, while the cage stood 6" high. The lamp is pictured here on the left next to the Vapo-Cresolene box.

The Jr. Rochester Stand Lamp

In its 1891-92 catalog, the Rochester Lamp Company offered the Jr. Rochester Stand Lamp in rolled polished brass or nickel, standing 8" high to the top of the burner, and a Jr. Rochester Hand Lamp standing 6¼" high. The latter came with a pretty, decorated glass ball shade. Offered with a glass, linen or silk shade, the Jr. Rochester Stand Lamp was recommended in the catalog as a "beautiful little lamp for college students, school rooms, professors and all who occupy their sleeping apartments more or less before retiring." A reprint of the Rochester catalog came courtesy of Dr. David Portman. Patented in 1886, the Jr. Rochester sometimes took a white glass umbrella shade, as shown here in the photo by Dean Langness of his lamp. Called the most convenient kitchen or bedroom lamp it was used in homes and hotels.

The most handsome metal lamps were the miniature brass student lamps. One just sold at auction for $1,250, bringing the highest price ever for such a lamp. In the collection of R. Wayne Hall, the brass double student lamp is shown here, although no company was located for it. What is known about student lamps? Arthur Peterson, in *400 Trademarks on Glass*, researched the patents and found that Carl Kleeman of Erfurt, Prussia, made the German Student Lamps or Kleeman lamps. Then after Kleeman's death in 1871, C.F.A. Hinrichs, his U.S. agent, obtained the registered trademark KLEEMAN and continued to offer the lamps. Hence, most of these full-size student lamps, or those marked Kleeman, were imported from Germany, beginning in 1863 when Hinrichs became the agent for Kleeman. Trade journal ads offered student lamps through Hinrichs, B.B. Schneider and the German Student Lamp Company.

Brass Double Student Lamp

70

The Little Jewel lamp of Ansonia Brass

Who made miniature student lamps? As we saw in Chapter II, the Bristol Brass and Clock Company of New York offered the New Student Night Lamp (S 83), a petite brass lamp in April, 1878. We can assume that Manhattan Brass Co., Bristol Brass, possibly Edward Miller and Co., all made small student lamps, though we have no proof or pictures of them. Three years of research yielded scant information on this topic.

The Manhattan Brass Company advertised 35 varieties of student lamps in C & G, October 13, 1898, and called them Perfection Student Lamps. Undoubtedly, one of the 35 varieties was a miniature student lamp. It is important to note that most student lamps were full-size table lamps. Those measuring 13 inches or less were considered miniature student lamps and were used as chamber lamps. How we wish that the companies had advertised and pictured their miniature brass student lamps!

The Ansonia Brass and Copper Company of New York presented the popular Little Jewel lamp July 16, 1891, in PGR. Like the Little Royal, it came as a harp or a bracket lamp. It was made of brass with a plain font, with one to three rings around it and a pierced foot. Note the pattern of diamonds and x's on the foot, just like the Little Royal. The Little Jewel lamp pictured here belongs to Mary Jane Clark. Collectors can rejoice in the variety of the myriad metal night lamps, from the Cottage to the Little Beauty to the Vapo-Cresolene and the student lamps. Most are reasonably priced and provide a poor man's alternative to the expensive colored glass night lamps.

McFaddin's Glow Thrift Lamp

Glow Night Lamps: S 628 and S 625

McFaddin's Glow Thrift Lamp (S 626)

# Chapter VIII
# One-Night Stands: Glow, Duncan, Hobbs

Some companies, such as the Glow Night Lamp Company, Hobbs Glass and George Duncan and Sons, made only a few night lamps that were advertised in the trade journals. There is no evidence elsewhere that they made more than two or three lamps.

The Glow Night Lamp Company of Boston, Mass., made the Glow Night Lamp, a lamp with the maker's name embossed on the base. It came in myriad colors: clear, milk glass, green, blue, purple, amber, ruby, and in two styles, a ribbed Style No. 1 (S 625) and an embossed daisy design Style No. 2 (S 628). The latter was either embossed colored glass or sheer opaline, embossed and sometimes painted with tiny daisies. Both Style 1 and 2 came in two-tone combinations, a clear base with a milk glass shade or a milk glass base with ruby shade, for example. The patent date was 1895, but the lamp was still sold in 1906. Ads claimed that the lamp burned 200 hours on a pint of fuel, had no smoke, no smell, no waste, consumed its own gas and never leaked. Made entirely of glass, even the burner and wick were glass. Lucky the collector who finds one today with the glass wick intact!

Glow Thrift Lamps were advertised after 1900 by H.G. McFaddin and Company of New York. This company, founded in 1874, was famous for its invention in 1909 of the Emeralite Desk Lamp. McFaddin and Company claimed that they recognized the merits of the Glow Night Lamp, and improved its construction and appearance to make the ideal light for any home. In the December 12, 1918 ad from PGBS shown here, McFaddin included four models of Glow Thrift lamps, (1) S 626, (2) a hanging lamp with a metal base and glass ribbed shade, (3) a candle lamp, and (4) a ribbed lamp like S 625. The hanging lamp is pictured here by Arthur Ronat on a wooden stand. McFaddin's lamps resembled closely the Glow Night Lamps and used the same name.

George Duncan and Sons of Pittsburgh, Pennslyvania, presented the Narrow Swirl Night Lamp, May 15, 1890, in PGR. It had a thick, swirled base and a matching umbrella shade. With it came several other pieces, three- to seven-inch rose-bowls and a salt bottle. Swirl patterns were popular in the 1890's. Established in 1866, George A. Duncan was one of the largest manufacturers of pattern glass. The company in 1884 organized a plant at Pittsburgh that employed 150 workmen. It made the famous Three Face pattern in acid-etched glass. In 1891, George Duncan

Duncan's Narrow Swirl Night Lamp

Glow Thrift Lamps, PGBS Dec. 12, 1918. Reproduced from the collection of the Library of Congress

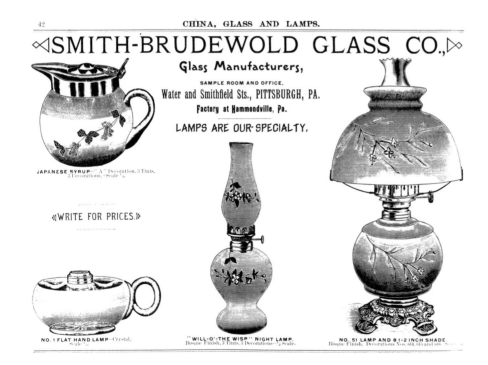

Will-O'-The Wisp Night Lamp, CGL. Aug. 17, 1892. Reproduced from the collection of the Library of Congress

74

joined the U.S. Glass Company and continued to make the Narrow Swirl Night Lamp. By 1894, with a new factory at Washington, Pennsylvania, the company left the USGC and became the Duncan and Miller Glass Company, with James E. Duncan as president. Noted for its pressed and blown tableware in crystal and colored glass, Duncan and Miller glass is very popular with collectors today (Kamm, V, pp. 93-95).

The Smith-Brudewold Glass Company of Pittsburgh offered the "Will-O'-The-Wisp" Night Lamp in *China, Glass and Lamps,* August 17, 1892. Made in a bisque finish, it came in three colors with three alternate decorations. As shown here in the ad, it had trailing apple blossoms painted on the base and shade.

The Opalescent Stripe Night Lamp by Hobbs. PGR May 15, 1890. Reproduced from the collection of the Library of Congress

Lamps, chandeliers and other lighting fixtures were produced in volume at Hobbs Glass Company, Wheeling, West Virginia, in the 1870's and 1880's. In June, 1886, the company acquired a patent for the "Manufacture of Opalescent Glassware." In his chapter on Hobbs in *American Pressed Glass,* Albert Christian Revi describes how opalescence occurred. A mold was made for the glass object, and on the face of the mold were indentations to form nodules on the surface of the article. Molten glass was pressed in the mold, then removed and cooled in a blast of air. Then it was reheated to a red hot heat to bring out the opalescent effects on the nodules. This is how the lovely Plain Windows Night Lamp (S 510), belonging

The Fairy Night Lamp by Richards and Hartley

Plain Windows (S 510) and two Opal Swirl lamps (S 512, 513) by Hobbs

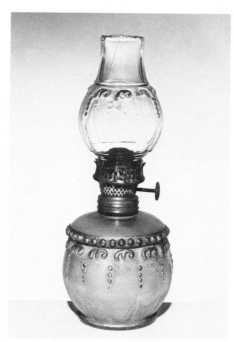

The Cuban Night Lamp by Ball, Deiters & Crowl

The Fishscale lamp by Buckeye

to Mary Jane Clark, was made. It came in crystal opalescent, sapphire opalescent and ruby opalescent, according to the reprint from the Hobbs 1890 catalog, shown in Heacock II, p. 114.

The Opalescent Stripe Night Lamp by Hobbs was advertised in PGR on May 15, 1890, in an ad reproduced here. This same lamp came also in an Opalescent Seaweed pattern S 508. Hobbs Glass made several opalescent night lamps: S 508, 510, 512, 513. Both the Plain Windows (S 510) and the Opalescent Swirl (S 513) lamps are pictured in a glorious ruby color in the middle of the book. The Opalescent Swirl lamp was in a pattern made originally at Hobbs, with continued production at other companies (Heacock III, p.43). The Plain Windows, the Opal Stripe and the Opalescent Swirl night lamps all had inverted opalescent pattern shades and fonts with clear pressed bases. They were made in clear, pink, red and blue glass with opalescence, truly beautiful artifacts of an excellent glassmaker!

Richard and Hartley Glass Company of Tarentum, Pennsylvania, offered the Fairy Night Lamp on May 1, 1890, in C & G. This lamp resembled a fairy lamp, and came in clear pattern glass with a flat-handled base and a pyramid-type shade covering the chimney. After the company merged into the U.S. Glass Company, the Fairy Night Lamp appeared as a product of U.S. Glass in their big, undated color catalog. The lamp is 6½" high.

The Buckeye Glass Company of Martins Ferry, Ohio, made the Fishscale lamp (S 116) in blue, amber, green, vaseline and clear glass. It was advertised February 11, 1886, in C & G, with a Fishscale pattern font, pedestal and base.

The Cuban Night Lamp (S 55) was offered by Ball, Deiters and Crowl of Wellsburg, West Virginia, in an ad in CGL, March 18, 1896. Made in clear painted glass, it was shown with matching salt and pepper shakers. The company was known for decorating and producing glassware. While few in number, the night lamps of Ball, Deiters and Crowl, Hobbs, Duncan and others were made with great skill and ingenuity.

The Delft and the Dresden by Pairpoint

S 330, 331 by Pairpoint

# Chapter IX

# Limited Production:
# Pairpoint, Cambridge, Webb

The companies that made only one, two or three night lamps often made splendid ones. Looking at the production of Pairpoint, Thomas Webb or Tiffany, we marvel at the elegance, grace and beauty of those individual endeavors. The art glass lamps mark one of the high points in the history of the night lamp. While many were made by English firms such as Webb or Stevens and Williams, American companies like Tiffany contributed also.

Five lamps attributable to the Pairpoint Glass Company of New Bedford, Massachusetts, were found: the Classic, Bounty, Dresden, Delft and McKinley lamps. The Classic (S 130) was a simple milk glass lamp with an umbrella shade and ribbed panels on base and shade. Originally, colorful pansies graced both parts, but they have disappeared from most of these lamps today. The Classic night lamp is pictured on a page from a Pairpoint catalog reproduced in George Avila's *The Pairpoint Glass Story*, p. 132. Two other night lamps are mentioned by Avila, the Dresden and the Delft. The Dresden measured nine inches high and had a panelled ball shade and base, decorated with graceful sprays of daisies. The Delft lamp featured a Dutch landscape scene with windmills and boats. Using the same molds and milk glass blanks, Pairpoint produced both lamps with their names signed on the base, the Delft decorated in blue, the Dresden in muted shades of red, blue, green, tan and brown (Avila, p. 239). On February 20, 1896, the Delft and Dresden lamps were advertised in C & G. Pictured was the Delft lamp.

Pairpoint also offered the McKinley lamp on October 1, 1896, in *Crockery and Glass*. With President McKinley's portrait emblazoned on the ball shade, this handsome lamp stood 14½″ high. This same lamp came with windmill scenes and with flowers like S 331 and 330, respectively. The McKinley lamp had rich brown colors, with gold dollar signs around the portrait of McKinley. What a marvelous example of political memorabilia and what a discovery for the lamp collector! The most stunning Pairpoint lamp was the Bounty (S 305) shown in color in the center of the book. Almost a foot tall with its Art Nouveau metal base, classic tapered font and pansy decorated ball shade, it recently sold at auction for $700! It is authenticated by the Pairpoint signature on the base.

A full page ad in CGL, October 21, 1891, heralded the Pear Night Lamp of Greensburg Glass Company of Greensburg, Pennsylvania. It was S 147 in clear pressed glass with a font shaped like a pear sitting on a saucer base. With its intricate patterned umbrella shade matching the pattern in the saucer base, it was a triumph of the glassmaker's art.

The Classic by Pairpoint

The Bounty by Pairpoint

The Pear Night Lamp by Greensburg

The Pan Am Exposition lamp by Hengerer

The Pan Am Exposition lamp (S 309) made by the William Hengerer Company of Buffalo, New York, was presented in C & G, April 11, 1901. In milk glass, the lamp featured maps of North and South America joined by girls linking hands, and was decorated in maroon, yellow, green and blue. It was the official souvenir night lamp of the Pan American Exposition in Buffalo in 1901, a tradesman's exposition featuring glass, pottery, aluminum utensils, hammocks and other retail goods.

The Cambridge Glass Company made two night lamps, the Duchess and the Countess. Shaped like S 175, the Duchess had panels on its base with swags of ferns and flowers between each panel, while the Countess had petite rows of ribbing on the rim and base and swags in the center. Both are pictured in clear glass in the undated Cambridge Glass Company catalog reprinted by the Welkers in *The Cambridge Glass Company*. Labelled Cambridge Nearcut, they were made between 1910 and 1920. Despite a search, I was unable to locate these lamps.

Imported Opaline night lamp

Some of the prettiest night lamps were imported from Europe, such as those Noe brought from Germany, discussed in Chapter VI. C.F.A. Hinrichs of New York specialized in imported art glass, student lamps and Bohemian glass lamps. He advertised widely in the trade journals some exquisite items like the opaline night lamp shown here. The Kenneth Fishers own this lamp and kindly provided the photo. The lamp came with a plain milk glass ball shade and a pedestal base with pink trim, flowers and butterflies. Hinrichs imported lamps like this one and called them Bohemian Night Lamps.

Art glass night lamps were made by English and American firms. Thomas Webb and Sons made Burmese glass lamps such as S 608 and 610, as well as cameo glass lamps like S 611. The greatest challenge to the glassmaker was fabricating the cameo glass lamps. He had to meld different colored layers of glass to each other, then carve through the outer layer or layers until his design came to the fore. Usually, English cameo glass lamps, such as the one illustrated here from the Smiths' collection, had a satin glass background with a layer of white glass on top. Here the artist carved away the white layer of glass against the red satin background to produce an exquisite design of morning glories and leaves. In expense and desirability, the English cameo lamps rank first.

English Cameo glass lamp

S 579 by Kempton and Son

English cameo glass night lamps were made by Stevens and Williams and Thomas Webb and Sons of Stourbridge, England (note S 611, 612, 617). Stevens and Williams of Brierly Hill, Staffordshire, England, registered S 612, a cameo lamp with a Maidenhair Fern design, in December, 1886, at the Design Registry Office in London, according to A.C. Revi in a *Spinning Wheel* article, March, 1974. It came in colored satin glass with detailed white relief carving of ferns.

Revi's article also mentions the British firm Kempton and Son who made the Verre Moire night lamp on a plush cloth base S 578, S 579 in red satin glass on a plush base and S 576 in Verre Moire. With mammoth ruffled umbrella shades, the first two lamps S 578 and 579 detach from their cloth bases that act as holders for the lamps. Illustrated here is S 579. Unfortunately, few art glass lamps were available to photograph.

Beautifully competitive with the art of the English glassmakers was L.C. Tiffany's Favrile night lamp (S 586). With its graceful gold Favrile umbrella shade, gold lustered base and chimney, it is fully signed L.C.T. and appears to be the only night lamp Tiffany made. Made up of five separate parts, it is sometimes found with one or more parts missing. We noted in earlier chapters that firms such as Gillinder and Consolidated produced beautiful colored satin glass lamps like the Pearl Baby McKee and the Rose night lamps. These are exceptional American art glass lamps, as is Tiffany's Favrile lamp. While few in number, the lamps of Pairpoint, Greensburg, Hengerer, Webb and Tiffany made a unique contribution to the evolution of the night lamp.

Tiffany Favrile lamp

S 105, the Optic, the Daisy and the Ribbed Pedestal lamps by USGC

# Chapter X

## The Combines: U.S. Glass Company and National Glass Company

In 1891, 15 glass companies merged to form the United States Glass Company. The aim of the merger was to increase profits through consolidating offices, to use a thorough purchasing system, to increase economical production and merchandising of glassware, and to expand into foreign markets. With Daniel C. Ripley as president, the new company began operation in the fall of 1891. A letter to their customers advised of the merger and requested that orders be sent to the U.S. Glass Company, with the name of the company that formerly made the goods. The original 15 companies included:

Adams and Company, Pittsburgh, Pa.
Bryce Brothers, Pittsburgh, Pa.
Bellaire Goblet Co., Findlay, Ohio
Central Glass Co., Wheeling, W.Va.
Columbia Glass Co., Findlay, Ohio
Challinor, Taylor and Co., Tarentum, Pa.
Doyle and Co., Pittsburgh, Pa.
George Duncan and Sons, Pittsburgh, Pa.
Gillinder and Sons, Greensburg, Pa.
Hobbs Glass Co., Wheeling, W. Va.
King Glass Co., Pittsburgh, Pa.
Nickel Plate Glass Co., Fostoria, Ohio
O'Hara Glass Co., Pittsburgh, Pa.
Richards & Hartley, Tarentum, Pa.
Ripley & Co., Pittsburgh, Pa.

Three more companies joined the U.S. Glass Co.: A.J. Beatty and Sons of Tiffin, Ohio, A.J. Beatty and Sons of Steubenville, Ohio, and the Novelty Glass Co., Fostoria, Ohio. This brought the membership to 18. Of these 18, some were destroyed by fire, others were sold or consolidated and left the USGC, according to Heacock and Bickenheuser, in *U.S. Glass from A to Z*, the source used for the history of USGC.

In early 1893, the company bought 500 acres of land on the Monongahela River near McKeesport, Pennsylvania, to establish a new plant. Eventually, a city sprouted around it, that was called Glassport, Pennsylvania. The years of 1892 and 1893 were tumultuous for the new merged company. There was a depression in the United States, and conflicts were brewing between the management and the American Flint Glass Workers Union. The company urged the Flint Glass workers to allow their members to work during the summer instead of shutting down for the usual six to eight weeks, to remove restrictions on worker output, to improve the production capacity of the various factories, and to produce competitive items such as beer mugs and tumblers at equal rates with competitors.

The union refused these requests, and on October 12, 1893, went on strike. The USGC brought in green help and continued to operate its factories, but nonetheless incurred large losses over the three-year period of the strike. This was not a strike for higher wages, but one for limits on production. Unable to harness the productivity of the USGC, the workers capitulated after three and a half years of semi-starvation, debt and useless protestation. On January 1, 1897, the American Flint Glass Workers Union gave up the fight and agreed to increase production.

By 1897, the company assigned different plants to manufacture certain types of glass. The Tiffin, Ohio, plant became a blown ware factory making lead blown tumblers, stemware and cut glass. Gas City, Indiana, became a pressed ware factory for tumblers, beer mugs, jellies, etc.

By 1900, only these factories of the original 18 were still operating: Adams and Company, Bryce Brothers, Ripley and Company, King Glass Company, Doyle and Company, and A.J. Beatty and Sons. The strike had caused considerable attrition, as did fires, sales and consolidations.

Was U.S. Glass involved in lamp production? Yes, it was from the time of the merger. By July, 1898, the company was showing 218 different styles and decorations of glass lamps, many of them developed originally by the member factories. The company continued to offer the Westmoreland night lamps of Gillinder and the Narrow Swirl lamp of Duncan.

Much of the pressed glassware offered by U.S. Glass was from molds of the member firms, since the company acquired the molds, patents and rights to produce the lamps and other glassware offered by these companies. Some of the most familiar night lamps made by U.S. Glass included the Daisy (S 112), the Stars and Bars (S 482), the Remington Night Lamp (S 150), the Sheraton (S 167) and the Bullseye (S 110). The Stars and Bars night lamp was made first by Bellaire Goblet, and subsequently offered by USGC. It appeared in the U.S. Glass Co. Catalog circa 1900, and is shown in color in the center of this book.

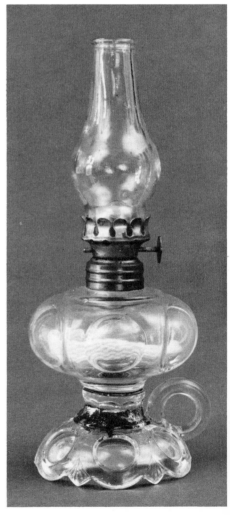

The handled Daisy by USGC

86

The 1909 USGC Catalog showed these lamps: the Swirl (S 475), the Daisy (S 112), the Optic (S 103), S 105, and the Ribbed Pedestal as numbered night lamps in the 9000 series. The catalog pictured the Swirl lamp (S 475) without a shade. The 1919 catalog featured the popular Sheraton or Grecian Key lamp (S 167). It came in green and clear glass. An ad in C & G on February 15, 1912, pictured the Bullseye lamp (S 110), a favorite, seemingly ubiquitous lamp. Patented in 1911, this lamp had the new screw-in glass collar. The ad warned competitors to respect the patent and threatened litigation for patent infringement. The glass collar was heralded as a new invention to prevent looseness and leakage.

The Bullseye, the Swirl and the Sheraton by USGC

The company also offered the Bullseye in an attractive hand lamp. Both lamps came in clear glass, sometimes with flashed red bullseyes as shown here. On April 28, 1910, C & G reported that USGC had introduced 42 new lamps, with night lamps included. By October 12, 1911, the company announced that all their lamps would feature the new glass collar as in the Bullseye lamp.

The Corning Museum of Glass Library had in its collection a large, color U.S. Glass catalog, missing at present. That catalog had pictures of lamps which were duplicated by Catherine Thuro, who kindly shared them with me. Among them were a number of night lamps. It is probable that the catalog was published shortly after the merger or sometime between 1891-1895, and that most of the lamps shown were made earlier by a member company. For example, the catalog illustrated several Westmoreland night lamps: S 144, 145, 146 by Gillinder and Sons. The Opal Stripe Night Lamp, a Hobbs' 1890 offering, was shown, as was George Duncan and Sons' Narrow Swirl Night Lamp of the same year. Richards and Hartley Glass Company's Fairy Night Lamp appeared with Bellaire Goblet's Stars and Bars (S 482).

Other lamps included S 52, the famous Match-holder lamp called the Happy Thought Night Lamp, offered in amber, blue or crystal; S 75, the Vestal Night Lamp with a shade like the Match-holder lamp. Smiths called this the Aladdin lamp. Also pictured were the Remington Night Lamp (S 150), another fairy type lamp in the Bullseye pattern; the Vivian night lamp, and the Stars and Bars Cigar Lighter lamp, the last two not available to photograph but shown in Thuro, p. 327. Other lamps mentioned here are pictured in the chapters on their company of origin; for example, the Westmoreland night lamps are in Chapter V on Gillinder and Sons. Shown in color in the middle of the book are the Stars and Bars and the Swirl lamp in blue glass, the Match-holder lamp in amber and the Remington Night Lamp in clear glass.

Butler Brothers in their Spring 1914 Catalog offered several night lamps by U.S. Glass including the Sheraton, the Swirl, S 105 and the Ribbed Pedestal. They also showed the popular Block and Dot lamps S 190, 191, and S 192, the Mission lamp. Butler Brothers called all these lamps Mission lamps, and the Block and Dot were named Mission Octagon. These milk glass and clear lamps were gaily decorated in pink, green and yellow, with black paint outlining each panel. Today, most of the paint has worn off. The Mission lamp (S 192) came originally with brightly colored flowers between gilt panels. I believe that all these Mission lamps were made

The Match-holder and the Remington Night lamps by USGC

The Mission lamp (S 192) and two Mission Octagon lamps (S 191 and 190) by USGC

by U.S. Glass, and base my proof on a statement in C & G, June 2, 1910: "A night lamp in mission effects has just been shown by U.S. Glass." The use of the words "Mission design" and "Mission Octagon" in Butler Brothers Spring 1914 Catalog and the presence in this catalog of several other lamps made by USGC seem to corroborate my theory. This is speculation, however, as none of these lamps is shown in U.S. Glass catalogs or ads.

The U.S. Glass Company prospered and grew. Like a chameleon, it changed its colors and designs to fit customer demand and current fashion. As oil lamps gave way to electric lamps, the company turned to electric lighting and produced some exquisite electric figural night lamps: the Parrot Lamp, the Love Bird, the Owl, the Fruit Basket, the Rabbit, the Crinoline Girl, the Flower Basket, the Flower Console and the Fruit Console Night Lamps. These were all pictured in *The Glass Outlook* in August, 1924, a promotion magazine published by USGC. Lighted from within by a small bulb, the lamps stood 9 to 12 inches high. They came in many colors; the owl in brown with an ebony base, the parrot in bright reds and greens. The glass was clear molded, then painted to look like the object. They resembled the early figural oil lamps, such as the Columbus and the Santa Claus. By October 14, 1926 in C & G the company offered a Santa Claus lamp showing Santa issuing from a chimney with a bag of toys. The Santa lamp decorated the hall or console table or sat under the tree during the holiday season. Pictured here by Elizabeth Trudell from her collection, Santa grins widely.

Why was such a figural lamp made? "It is designed to lend a touch of the unusual to the living room, library or nursery. It will make a unique gift and will receive a welcome when distributed as a prize at bridge," claimed the ad in C & G, May 10, 1923. These lamps can be found and purchased rather reasonably today, and make a fine addition to a night lamp collection. Are they truly night lamps? Yes, they are. As we saw above, they were used in the nursery. They represent the final act in this fascinating drama of tiny lamps.

The National Glass Company, formed in 1899, was an amalgamation of 19 glass companies including Greensburg Glass, Northwood Glass, Dalzell, Gilmore and Leighton, and several others. The president, H.C. Fry, and the U.S. Glass Company president, Daniel Ripley, worked to control the prices of blown and pressed tableware, since the two corporations produced 85% of the tableware in the United States. The National Glass company did not achieve the success that the U.S. Glass Company enjoyed. Indeed, by 1902, several factories had resigned or

The Electric Owl Night Lamp by USGC

closed down, and only 12 of the 19 factories remained in the company, Revi points out in *American Pressed Glass.* By 1903, the firm was financially unstable, and H.C. Fry had left to open his own factory. Despite a reorganization and a new stock issue in 1903, the corporation was defunct by 1904.

The National Glass Company, operating Dalzell, Gilmore and Leighton Glass Works, advertised a Dakota Night Lamp, May 2, 1902, in CGL. The ad is reprinted in Chapter IV. We can assume that some night lamps produced by Dalzell, Greensburg, and the other glass companies in the combine were re-offered by the National Glass Co. This certainly occurred with USGC, as we have seen. Both the U.S. Glass Co. and National Glass Co. contributed to the development of the night lamp, and both made possible the continued offering of these lamps into the first two decades of the 20th century.

The Santa and the Owl by USGC

The Plume Milk Glass Satin, the Beaded Milk Glass and Fluted Pink Toy Rose by Wright

# Chapter XI
# New Night Lamps

Astute collectors of night lamps would do well to buy all the new ones they can find. It is useful to have the new ones to compare and to contrast with the old. Further, some of the new ones are beautifully made in rich colors. The work of the L.G. Wright Company is commendable. Wright contracts with various glass companies, for example Fenton or Viking, to make certain lamps. Among their offerings in the Master Catalog under Toy Lamps are the Beaded Ruby, Plume Ruby Satin, Plume Ruby, Fluted Ruby, Beaded Ruby Satin, Beaded Milk Glass, Beaded Milk Glass Satin, Plume Milk Glass Satin, the Fluted Buttercup, Fluted Pink Toy Rose, Fluted Desert Rose. These are exquisite miniature lamps, some of which may come from the original molds, with umbrella and ball shades. The Plume lamps are nearly identical to the old Plume lamp (S 203), while the Beaded lamps resemble the old Beaded Drape lamp (S 400).

I was fortunate to get photos of the following Wright lamps: the Plume Satin with Amber Overlay and the Daisy and Cube, shown with its old counterpart, the Stars and Bars Lamp (S 482). Just before going to press, I bought three Wright lamps photographed here: the Plume Milk Glass Satin, the Beaded Milk Glass and the Fluted Pink Toy Rose. These lamps retail at $30.50 to $40.50 for the hand painted Pink Toy Rose. They are the finest new night lamps currently on the market and may be purchased from gift shops that sell Wright products. The Plume Milk Glass Satin lamp differs from the old lamp in color and composition. The old Plume Lamp (S 203) came in milk glass with gilt paint; its design of swirled plumes was distinctive and detailed. The new lamps come in ruby glass, amber, white, blue and rose satin glass, colors inimical to the old lamp. Wright no longer offers the Plume Satin Amber, Rose or Blue Overlay lamps.

It is difficult to distinguish between the old and the new Beaded Drape lamps. The old Beaded Drape (S 400) was made in red, blue, green and pink satin glass. In the Master Catalog of the Wright Company, the new lamp is offered in these colors and finishes: Beaded Ruby and Beaded Ruby Satin; Beaded Milk Glass and Beaded Milk Glass Satin, and Beaded Satin with Amber Overlay. So, the new Beaded Drape lamps exist in red, white, amber and possibly pink satin glass. Caveat emptor! The lamp pictured here on the right, the Fluted Pink Toy Rose, is not a reproduction of an old lamp. With its melon ribs, it has a satin texture and delicately painted pink roses, artist signed Marie.

The old Stars and Bars lamp with the new amberina Daisy and Cube by Wright

The Cranberry Opal Dot with ball shade by Wright

Currently, Wright offers all the lamps in the Master Catalog except the Cranberry Opal Dot, Cranberry Honeycomb and Cranberry Thumbprint with umbrella shades, the Daisy and Cube (S 482) lamps, the Beaded Satin and the Plume Satin with Amber Overlay. Look for these lamps to appreciate rather quickly. A recent list of lamps for sale priced the discontinued Wright lamps at $95 to $175, which seems exorbitant!

Wright did offer the Daisy and Cube or Stars and Bars (S 482) lamp in milk glass, amberina, amber and green. The old lamp came in clear, amber and blue. Beware of the amber lamps! The Wright inverted shade was taller than the old Bellaire shade and the font more rounded. Note the two lamps pictured together here, the old blue one on the left, the new amberina one on the right.

At the moment, Wright offers a Moon and Star lamp with a pedestal base and an umbrella shade in blue, amber and ruby. The old Moon and Star lamp base, shown here in clear glass, may once have had a shade. It is identical in shape, size and pattern to the new blue Moon and Star lamp which measures 8″ high to the top of its umbrella shade. Possibly the old lamp came only in clear glass. So, color could be a guide.

Another lamp currently in stock is the Cranberry Opal Dot with ball shade, standing 8½″ high to the top of its large ball shade. There is no old lamp similar to it. It is unique, costly, and difficult to make, retailing for more than $50.00. Few American glassmakers make cranberry glass today. The company also sells a Cranberry Thumbprint lamp with ball shade and most of the other lamps on page 76 of the Master Catalog, including the Plume, the Beaded Drape and the Fluted lamps. Master Catalogs are very scarce and only a few gift shop owners have them.

Perhaps most confusing to collectors are the Cranberry Opal Dot and Cranberry Thumbprint lamps with umbrella shades, which closely resemble S 434. Two years ago, I purchased the Cranberry Opal Dot lamp at a high price, thinking it was old and later had to return it for a refund. While these lamps with umbrella shades are no longer made by Wright, they are still new lamps.

In summary, collectors should examine carefully any lamps similar to S 203, 400, 434 or 482, noting the colors that old lamps came in and the photos of the old lamps here. Pictured in color here are the new Wright Plume lamp with amber overlay and the old Fostoria Plume lamp. It would be wise to compare the two carefully. A mistake of $25 to $50 is not a bad mistake, but to pay $200 to $500 for a new Wright lamp is a gross error!

The new Moon and Star lamp by Wright

The old Moon and Star lamp

The A. A. Importing Company of St. Louis, Missouri, offered four miniature lamps in their 1973 catalog. Two look very new indeed, and have no pattern. Measuring 9″ high, they come in blue and red stained glass, one with a simple ball shade and oval base, the other with a pedestal base and umbrella shade. These lamps should not confuse collectors. The Daisy and Button and Star and Panel lamps look older. I purchased both recently to include them here and in color in the middle of the book. The blue on these lamps is a shade of blue never found in old lamps. All four lamps come in clear glass stained blue and red.

Shown on the next page from left to right are the old Daisy and Button with Thumbprint (S 419) in milk glass, the new blue Daisy and Button by A.A. Importing, the blue Star and Panel by A.A., and the amber Plume by Wright. The old Daisy and Button with Thumbprint lamp (S 419) was first made by Adams and Company of Pittsburgh, before 1891, in milk glass with pink trim and in lustrous white. The new lamp came only in blue and red. Comparing the old with the new Daisy and Button lamp, I found (1) the old lamp was 8″ high, the new 9″ high to the top of the shade, (2) the umbrella shade in the old lamp rested on a spider, while in the new it rested on a circular metal disc fitting over the chimney, (3) the diameter of the shade in the old was 4″, while in the new it was 4½″, (4) the shade in the old had a bell tone when tapped lightly, while the new one had a dull tone, and (5) the old lamp had an old Nutmeg burner while the new one had the typical new burner common to reproductions.

The Star and Panel lamp, third from left, was also offered by A.A. Importing in 1973. It had a large, inverted shade with a ruffled top. The base had a variety of patterns from a star under the collar to panels separated by crimping to beads and diamonds, entirely too rococo. The lamps by A.A. Importing were not as well made as the Wright lamps and should not confound the collector. The 1978 catalog contained no miniature lamps, but those offered in 1973 are still available. The two shown here were purchased in May, 1978.

The old and new Daisy and Button with Thumbprint lamps, the Star and Panel and the amber Plume lamp by Wright

Imperial Glass Corporation of Bellaire, Ohio, makes some handsome night lamps today. For the Bicentennial, they offered their Americana Collection, Handcrafted Reproductions of Old Lamps. These included a Boutique lamp in the grape pattern which came in several colors, yellow, blue, green, and featured clusters of grapes and leaves on the base with a clear chimney. In their 1962 catalog, Imperial pictured the Boutique lamps in clear glass, milk glass, amber, blue, mustard and sueded crystal. It is possible that the milk glass Boutique lamps were made also in 1950, since this date appears below the photo. The milk glass lamps had matching milk glass chimneys. I have not seen these offered in 1978, but did purchase the Boutique lamps in mustard and deep blue recently. They are pictured here and in color in the middle of the book.

The Boutique lamps by Imperial on each end with the new Fleur-de-Lis lamps in green and blue in the center

The Bundling lamp is shown also in the 1962 Imperial catalog and may be purchased today. In 1962, it came in milk glass, sueded crystal, mustard, antique blue, heather, decorated ruby and amber. By 1978, the company made the lamp in green glass also. Often this lamp is priced very high at antiques shows, but it dates 1962-1978 and should retail at $25 or less.

Was there an old Bundling lamp? Yes, indeed, the Bundling lamp was Imperial Number 9 (Kamm VII, p. 61). Kamm states that it was made in 1904-1905, and came in a low-handled kerosene lamp with a matching shade. The new Bundling lamps are reproductions of Imperial No. 9. In the photo, compare the old clear lamp on the right sans shade with the new green one on the left. The old crystal lamp is much lighter in weight than the new; the pattern is more pronounced. Between the leaf-like projections are collections of six-sided hobs, 12 in all, sharp to the touch in the old lamp, smoother and duller in the new one. In the old lamp, the leaf projections are rounded into an oval below the collar and apron while in the new lamp they are left unfinished. The new lamp is slightly taller, almost a half-inch taller than the old lamp. The old lamp came only in clear glass.

The new Bundling lamps appear in a variety of colors as noted above. If the collector finds a colored Bundling lamp, he can assume it is new. Apparently the lamp sells well, since Imperial continues to reproduce it year after year. Special thanks goes to Lucile Kennedy of Imperial Glass for sharing copies of Imperial's 1962 catalog. The Bundling lamps, Boutique lamps and Fleur-de-Lis lamps are pictured in color in the middle of the book.

In May, 1978, I purchased the Fleur-de-Lis lamp (S 228) in cobalt blue. I do not know which company reproduced this lamp, but suspect it was Imperial Glass, since the quality is so fine and the burners are marked Abco Nutmeg as on the Boutique and Bundling lamps. The old lamp never came in colored glass, such as cobalt or pale green shown here.

Produced by Eagle Glass, the old Fleur-de-Lis was made in clear and milk glass with the embossed fleur-de-lis outlined boldly in black, red or gold. The reproduction is so well made that it often deceives collectors, who think it is old when they see it priced at more than $200 at an antiques show. "Never buy blue" is the motto with this lamp! In fact, avoid all colored lamps in this pattern.

In summary, the new lamps make an attractive and inexpensive addition to a night lamp collection. They may be found in gift shops and purchased for $10 to $40. Undoubtedly, they will grow in value and scarcity as the old lamps have.

The new Bundling lamp and the old Imperial No. 9 lamp both by Imperial Glass

The Apple Blossom lamp by Northwood

# Chapter XII

# Conjectures and Conclusions:
# Northwood to Beaumont

Presumably, Harry Northwood made some night lamps during his long career as a glassmaker, but none are pictured in catalogs or trade journal ads. They say his glass was so popular and sold so well that he rarely needed to advertise. The Northwood Company is noted for certain patterns unique to it, and some of these patterns are found in night lamps. So, we may surmise that Northwood made certain night lamps. In this chapter, attribution is based on pattern and conjecture.

Harry Northwood had a long and distinguished career as a glassmaker. He came to America from England in 1885, worked for and managed several glass companies. First he worked for LaBelle Glass Company in Bridgeport, Ohio, and was manager of the plant in 1887, when the firm closed. Thereafter, he moved to Buckeye Glass Co. at Martins Ferry, Ohio, and remained associated with them until 1896, even while lending his name to another firm in Martins Ferry. This firm made glass in many colors, while the Buckeye firm made only crystal (Kamm V, p. 88). From Martins Ferry, Northwood's company moved to Elwood, Pennsylvania, in 1895, and later to Indiana, Pennsylvania, by 1896. Here the firm became The Northwood Company, and later The Northwood Glass Works. The company joined the National Glass Co. in 1899, but resigned in 1902. In 1902, Northwood bought the old plant of Hobbs, Brockunier and Co. at Wheeling. As was announced in *Crockery & Glass* on May 22, "Harry Northwood and Co. will be operating one of the furnaces at the old Hobbs, Brockunier plant this fall in the production of colored glassware, novelties and specialties." Here the name changed again to Northwood and Company and production included colored glass novelties, pressed tableware, colored glass with opalescent rims, and gilded, pressed crystal. Few ads exist to document lines, patterns, shapes or items made by Northwood. In 1905, the famous Northwood trademark appeared, the N in a circle. By 1910, the firm became The Harry Northwood Glass Company at Wheeling and advertised the famous iridescent glass known now as Carnival Glass.

William Heacock points out that Northwood was at the Indiana, Pennsylvania, site from 1896 to 1902, and that the factory continued to carry his name until 1904, when it became the Dugan Glass Co., run by Northwood's uncle. The connection between the Northwood-Dugan companies was very close and the latter company may have done sub-contract work for Northwood, Heacock claims in Book IV, pp. 12-13. Heacock bases his proof that Northwood made certain lines on shards dug up at the Indiana factory site. Several factories, however, did use this site. The

Northwood's Royal Ivy (S 431), S 294, Spanish Lace (S 471) and Quilted Phlox (S 388) lamps

Dugan Glass Company made night lamps here, and had eight on the market January 12, 1907, all "nobby little affairs," according to C & G. Witness Crocodile Tears (S 257), which Heacock attributes to Dugan (IV, p. 57).

Knowledge of typical Northwood patterns leads to the conclusion that the company did make the Royal Ivy night lamp (S 431) and the Apple Blossom lamp (S 195). The Royal Ivy pattern was assigned to Northwood by Kamm (V, p. 87) and other glass researchers. William Heacock attributed the Apple Blossom pattern to Northwood, basing his proof on an ad April 29, 1896, in *China, Glass and Lamps.* This journal provides much information on Apple Blossom, especially in an article April 15, 1896, on "Pennsylvania." "The factory of the Northwood Co., Indiana, is putting one of the handsomest fine blown tableware sets on the market at present that we have seen for many a day. Made in fine lead opal, graceful as artistic blown goods only can be, with an apple blossom in relief, hand painted and tinted, this line is sure to prove a leader. . . . a new line of artistic opal decorated lamps are in preparation."

Following this announcement, Northwood ran an ad on April 29, 1896, in CGL: "Apple Blossom is the new line of Artistic, Fine, Blown, Lead, Opal Tableware. Apple Blossom is relief decorated, acknowledged the finest blown tableware set now on the market." On May 13, 1896, the company announced, "New Line of Lamps Now Ready" in the Apple Blossom pattern. Considering this substantial promotional campaign with its fine description of the line, we can attribute S 195, the Apple Blossom lamp, to Northwood.

Another Northwood pattern is Parian Ruby, which swirled clockwise from left to right on each piece, and came in red and blue satin glass with crude enameled flowers on the upper part of the body. It was made in a table set, pitcher, tumbler, berry bowl, salt, toothpick and night lamp, according to Kamm, V, p. 89. Parian Ruby appears to be the pattern on S 293, since the lamp has a swirl pattern with the swirls going clockwise and a decoration of enameled daisies. Hence, we can ascribe S 293 to Northwood. A twin to the Parian Ruby lamp is S 294 shown here in spatter glass. Both lamps were made from the same mold by the same company. Therefore, we can also assign S 294 to Northwood.

William Heacock attributes S 388, the Quilted Phlox night lamp, to Northwood in Book III, p. 37. This lovely lamp came in cased colors of green, pink and blue, and resembled the Florette pattern made by Kopp. Heacock believes that Northwood and Dugan Glass made Quilted Phlox at the Indiana, Pennsylvania, plant sometime between 1894 and 1905.

Northwood also made a lovely Spanish Lace night lamp (S 471) in cranberry, vaseline and blue glass. William Heacock believes that the pattern was made first in Britain's Stourbridge area, and copied by Northwood over a number of years at his U.S. factories from 1885 to 1920 (III, p. 41 and II, p. 45). Heacock claims that Northwood made the Spanish Lace pattern in a water set, table set, berry set, syrup jug, sugar shaker, miniature lamp, etc., at Buckeye and Indiana, Pennsylvania. Studying the exquisite picture in Heacock's Book III, p. 41 of the salt shaker in cranberry Spanish Lace, we find that it corresponds perfectly to the pattern in Smith 471, and can therefore attribute S 471 to Northwood.

A detailed study of Heacock's patterns in Book III, *Victorian Colored Pattern Glass*, yields some other attributions. Again note that these lamps were not documented by trade journal ads, but by studying patterns in Heacock's book and comparing them with the patterns on night lamps. Therefore, they belong in this chapter of conjectures, rather than in chapters containing positive attributions. Heacock believes that the pattern Utopia Optic was produced at either Northwood or Buckeye Glass plants. In Book III, p. 44, he shows a beautiful green Utopia Optic ribbed syrup, with delicate enameled daisies and circles of dots. This pattern matches that on S 470 night lamp. Produced circa 1892, Utopia Optic came in decorated green and blue glass in a syrup, sugar shaker and night lamp.

The Belmont Glass Company probably made S 480 in the Reflecting Fans pattern (Heacock III, p. 54). It came in crystal, amber and blue glass and was made at Bellaire, Ohio, around 1885. Heacock found it only in a cruet. The same pattern, however, appears on the lamp S 480. Hence we can attribute S 480 to Belmont and call it "Reflecting Fans".

The Cooperative Flint Glass Company made the Famous pattern, circa 1899, in crystal, apple green and ruby stained glass. It is pictured in Heacock's Book III, p.

The Utopia Optic lamp by Northwood or Buckeye

Reflecting Fans lamp by Belmont

23 in a syrup. If we compare the night lamp S 478 to the syrup, we see that they are the same pattern. Hence we can ascribe S 478 to Cooperative Flint and call it the Famous night lamp. This lamp and a larger table lamp have been found only in clear glass.

Who made the Acorn night lamp (S 121)? This charming lamp shaped exactly like an acorn was produced by the Beaumont Glass Company, Martins Ferry, Ohio, circa 1890-1900. The pattern on the lamp resembles exactly that on the syrup and sugar shaker shown in Heacock, Book III, p. 14. Delicately ribbed in an opal stripe pattern with a stippled base, the lamp came in several colors. We are grateful for William Heacock's research and findings in the colored pattern glass field. With the aid of his books, we were able to match several night lamps with their companies of origin.

In conclusion, we have seen how the demand for decorated oil lamps was not just a passing fashion, but endured for several decades. Compared to the overly bright glare of the electric light and the flickering gas light, the soft, steady glow of the oil lamp seemed better and cheaper. Women could carry their lamps in hand from room to room, and hence found the oil lamp the ideal way to light the home. Even with bitter competition from the gas and electric companies, the oil lamp reigned supreme at the turn of the century. The manufacturers responded to the public taste, perfected the burners, the chimneys, and produced a gorgeous array of painted, decorated, cased, colored and opaline lamps. There seemed to be no limit to the imagination of the glassmaker, and the night lamp grew and thrived, providing us today with a treasury of beauty.

It must have been not only popular  but also profitable for the companies to produce night lamps. They were found in children's bedrooms, in halls, bathrooms, on the lady's desk and dressing table. They were offered as salesmen's samples or as small replicas of the larger lamps. For example, both the Crown and the Cosmos lamps came in both full-size lamps and night lamps.

To most collectors, attribution is very important. They would rather know who made the lamp and when than possess any other information about it. It's a delight to picture the gaffers of old blowing the early chamber lamps, to imagine the European immigrant glassmakers domiciled in Pennsylvania dreaming of new colors, fanciful flowers, fruits and cherub decorations, to visualize Nicholas Kopp creating his bright Kopp colors.

The Famous night lamp by Cooperative Flint

For me, night lamps have become a beacon to illuminate the past. I enjoy contemplating our ancestors, yours and mine, progressing from the purely functional Betty lamps to the simple classical whale oil lights, arriving at last at the most beautiful lamps of all, the Victorian night lamps with their enchanting colors, finishes and decorations from the lovely pale pink satin glass Rose lamp of Fostoria Shade to the sparkling Westmoreland lamp of Gillinder. In a sense, America flexed her muscle, industrially and artistically, in the production of her night lamps.

The Acorn lamp by Beaumont

Ann Gilbert McDonald is a writer and antiques dealer. She has written articles for *Antiques Observer, Antique Trader Weekly, Collectors News* and *Pottery Collectors Newsletter.* She received her doctorate in literature in 1969 and subsequently taught at Georgetown University. Living in Virginia with her husband Bradley, an attorney, and her eight-year-old son Perry, she is active in community affairs and teaches writing to Madison Center Senior Adults.

# Bibliography

Antique Trader Weekly. *Annual of Articles.* Vols. II-VII. Dubuque, Iowa, 1973-1977.

American Historical Catalog Collection. *Lamps and Other Lighting Devices 1850-1906.* Princeton: The Pyne Press, 1972.

Avila, George. *The Pairpoint Glass Story.* New Bedford, Massachusetts, 1968.

Bassett, Preston. "The Evolution of the American Glass Lamp," *The Rushlight,* 33 (Feb. 1967), pp. 5-12.

Belknap, E. McCamly. *Milk Glass.* New York: Crown Publishers, 1949.

Cooke, Lawrence S. *Lighting in America. From Colonial Rushlights to Victorian Chandeliers.* New York: Universe Books, 1975.

Delmore, Mrs. Edward J. *Victorian Miniature Oil Lamps.* Manchester, Vermont: Forward's Color Productions, 1968.

Golden, Grace. "Miniature Glass Lamps," *Hobbies,* 58 (Sept. 1953), pp. 114-115.

Hayward, Arthur H. *Colonial Lighting.* New York: Dover Publications, Inc., 1962.

Heacock, William. *Encyclopedia of Victorian Colored Pattern Glass.* Books I-V. Marietta, Ohio, 1974-78.

Innes, Lowell. *Pittsburgh Glass 1797-1891.* Boston: Houghton Mifflin Co., 1976.

Kamm, Minnie Watson. *Pitcher Books.* Vols. I-VIII. Detroit and Grosse Point, Michigan, 1939-1953.

Kearney, Virginia A. "A Review of Three Periods of American Glass Chamber and Night Lamps, with New Light on the 'Glow' Night Lamp," *Hobbies,* 62 (Feb. 1958), pp. 72-74.

Keyes, Willard Emerson. "Miniature Glass Lamps," *Antiques,* 32 (Sept. 1927), pp. 125-127.

Murray, Melvin K. *History of Fostoria, Ohio Glass 1887-1920.* Fostoria Ohio: Gray Printing Co., 1972.

Parvin, Edna M. "Miniature Lamps," *Hobbies,* 77 (April 1972), pp. 178-180.

Peterson, Arthur G. "Lamp Patents in the United States, Part I," *Hobbies,* 68 (July 1963), *pp. 82-83.*

_____ "Lamp Patents in the United States, Part II," *Hobbies,* 68 (Aug. 1963), pp. 82-85.

_____*400 Trademarks on Glass.* DeBary, Fla., 1968.

Revi, Albert Christian. "More Registered Designs for Fairy Lamps," *Spinning Wheel,* 30 (Mar. 1974), pp. 22-23.

_____*American Pressed Glass and Figural Bottles.* New York: Thomas Nelson and Sons, 1964.

Robinson, Marie. "Consolidated Lamp and Glass Company, Coraopolis, Pa.," *Spinning Wheel,* 30 (Mar. 1974), pp. 48-50.

Rollins, E.B. "Kerosene Lamps in the Average New England Home in 1880-1890s," *The Rushlight,* 21 (May 1955), pp. 5-10.

The Rushlight Club. *Early Lighting, A Pictorial Guide.* Boston, Massachusetts. The Rushlight Club, 1972.

Russell, Loris S. *A Heritage of Light.* Toronto: University of Toronto Press, 1968.

Shadel, Jane. "Glass Lighting Devices," *Antiques,* 98 (Dec. 1970), pp. 916-921.

Smith, Don E. *Findlay Pattern Glass.* Fostoria, Ohio: Gray Printing Co., 1970.

Smith, Frank R. and Ruth E. *Miniature Lamps.* New York: Thomas Nelson and Sons,, 1968.

Thuro, Catherine M.V. *Oil Lamps, The Kerosene Era in North America.* Des Moines, Iowa: Wallace-Homestead Book Co., 1976.

Thwing, Leroy and Julius Daniels. *A Dictionary of Old Lamps and Other Lighting Devices.* Cambridge, Massachusetts, 1952.

Van Pelt, Mary. *Figurines in Crystal.* 1975.

Watkins, Lura Woodside. "American Glass Lamps," *Antiques,* 29 (Apr. 1936), pp. 142-146.

_____*American Glass and Glassmaking.* London: Max Parrish and Co., 1950.

Watkins, Malcolm. "A Lamp Dealer Illustrates His Wares," *Antiques,* 35 (June 1939), pp. 297-299.

Weatherman, Hazel M. *Fostoria, Its First Fifty Years.* Springfield, Missouri, 1972.

Welker, Lyle, Mary, Lynn. *The Cambridge Glass Company.* Newark, Ohio: The Spencer Walker Press, 1974.

Wyant, Major L. B. "The Etiquette of Nineteenth Century Lamps," *Antiques,* 30 (Sept. 1936), pp. 113-117.

"New Home of the Consolidated Lamp and Glass Co.," *China, Glass and Lamps,* 7 (Feb. 28, 1894), p. 19.

"Lamps for My Lady's Desk," *"China, Glass and Lamps,* 8 (Nov. 14, 1894), p. 19.

"Pennsylvania," *China, Glass and Lamps,* 11 (April 15, 1896), p. 14.

"The Lamp Makers of America," *China, Glass and Lamps,* 11 (June 10, 1896), p. 14.

"A Swinging Success," *China, Glass and Lamps,* 12 (July 8 ,1896), p. 15.

"The Glass and Pottery Exhibit," *China, Glass and Lamps,* 26 (Jan. 12, 1907), pp. 6-13.

"The Lamp Trade," *Crockery and Glass Journal,* 27 (April 21, 1898), p. 16.

"Around the District," *Crockery and Glass Journal,* 59 (April 21, 1904), p. 20.

"The Exposition at Pittsburgh," *Crockery and Glass Journal,* 77 (June 23, 1913), p. 14.

"Illuminating Devices," *Crockery and Glass Journal,"* 81 (April 22, 1915), p. 11.

"William R. Noe Dies Suddenly," *Crockery and Glass Journal,"* 91 (May 6, 1920), p. 13.

"Household Utilities," *Crockery and Glass Journal,"* 92 (Nov. 4, 1920), p. 26.

"Observations on Lamps," *House Furnisher,* 9 (Aug. 1901), p. 22.

"Obituary of Nicholas Kopp," *The New York Times,* April 17, 1937, p. 17.

"W.A.B. Dalzell is Dead," *Pottery, Glass and Brass Salesman, 37 (Mar. 15, 1928), p. 9.*

"Glass Manufacturer's Exhibition," *Pottery and Glassware Reporter,* 24 (Jan. 15, 1891), pp. 12a-16a.

"The American Lamp of 1892," *Pottery and Glassware Reporter,* 26 (Feb. 18, 1892), pp. 12-15.

"Something About Lamps,"*Pottery and Glassware Reporter,* 25 (October 1, 1891), p. 16.

"Toilet Lamp for Dressing Table," *Pottery and Glassware Reporter,* 26 (March 1892), bis 3.

"The Lamp Season of 1892," *Pottery and Glassware Reporter,* 27 (April 14, 1892), bis 2.

"Lamps Increase Profit," *Pottery and Glassware Reporter,* 27 (Sept. 15, 1892), bis 2.

Glass Company Catalogs

Atterbury and Company 1872, 1881 catalogs.

Consolidated Lamp and Glass Company Catalog c. 1900.

Consolidated Lamp and Glass Company Catalog c. 1902.

Fostoria Catalog No. 4, Machine Made Lamps c. 1890.

Plume and Atwood Manufacturing Company Illustrated Catalogue. c. 1906 Reprinted by J.W. Courter Enterprises, Simpson, Illinois.

U.S. Glass Company. *The Glass Outlook,* 1 (August 1924).

U.S. Glass Company Catalog 1909.

U.S. Glass Company Catalog 1919.

The Rochester Lamp Company Catalog. New York 1891-92. Reprinted by Dr. David Portman, Gilded Age Press, Washington Mills, New York.

# Index